COMPILED AND EDITED BY
Judith Ferguson

RECIPES WRITTEN BY
Anne Ager, Judith Ferguson, Carolyn Garner,
Mary McCall, Denise Jarrett Macauley and
Mary Walsh

PHOTOGRAPHY BY
Peter Barry

DESIGNED BY
Sara Cooper

CLB 1668
This 1994 edition published by Magna Books
Magna Road, Wigston, Leicester LE18 4ZH
© 1987 CLB Publishing, Godalming, Surrey
All rights reserved
Printed and bound in Singapore
ISBN 1-85422-630-4

The recipes for Truffles and Mocha Ice Cream are the
copyright of Jennie Reekee and are reproduced by kind
permission of Ward Lock Ltd.

ITALIAN
COOKING

MAGNA
BOOKS

ITALIAN COOKING

CONTENTS

INTRODUCTION

What is your impression of Italian-style cooking? If the term conjures up mouthwatering images of the banquets that were characteristic of the days of the Roman Empire, when 'delicacies' such as whole sheep stuffed with oysters and dormice rolled in honey and poppy seed were popular fare, then you will be sadly disillusioned by present-day Italian cuisine.

Or, if you believe that pasta and pizza are the staple diet of the average Italian family, then you will be surprised as you browse through these recipes, or enjoy a meal in a traditional Italian restaurant, to appreciate the variety of flavours, colours and textures that give Italian cuisine its distinctive characteristics.

History books tell us that the Italians have always been fond of good food, though after the fall of the Roman Empire this interest waned. It was not until the Renaissance that the enjoyment of food again became an important feature of everyday life, and the style had changed. Quality, not quantity, became paramount. The Italians realised that they were blessed with a sun-drenched, fairly fertile country almost surrounded by sea. These geographical conditions undoubtedly influenced the style of Italian cooking.

Some ingredients and methods are peculiar to a particular area. Until 1861 Italy was composed of a number of separate states, each with its own geographic variations, traditions, lifestyles and government. Although now united under one government, many differences still remain. For example, fish cooking is prevalent in Liguria, a coastal state, while Bologna is a fertile area where dairy products predominate. In contrast, Abruzzi is a relatively infertile region where peppers are nevertheless plentiful, while Neapolitan-style cooking is characterised by the use of tomatoes, garlic, onions and olive oil.

The staple crops of Italy are rice and wheat. Rice is grown in the north of Italy, where rainfall is high and summers are hot – ideal conditions for the cultivation of rice. Consequently, risotto has become the traditional dish of northern Italy. Further south, the land and climate are more suited to the cultivation of wheat. The most successful variety is durum wheat. This type of wheat is hard, has a high protein content and is particularly suited to the making of pasta and pizza dough.

The main characteristics of Italian cooking are:

★ The abundant use of fresh vegetables native to Italy tomatoes, olives, peppers, aubergines, artichokes and courgettes

★ The subtle use of aromatic herbs such as basil, sage, rosemary, thyme, mint, parsley and bay leaf

★ The lavish and colourful use of native fruits: melons, apricots, pears, peaches and cherries, as well as nuts such as almonds and pistachios

Most importantly, if you eat 'Italian style', whether at a family meal, when entertaining friends or in an Italian restaurant, the meal is a social event. Italian life is very family oriented – mealtimes are occasions when people meet and talk. It may be a leisurely lunch followed by 'siesta', or a later meal in the cool of the evening. The food is usually accompanied by local Italian wines or carbonated water. The menu may include soup, most probably 'antipasta' (hors d'oeuvres – with a selection of cold meats and vegetables), pasta, risotto and a wide variety of salads, possibly a meat dish (often veal or chicken), and usually fresh fruit or a piece of cheese to round off the meal.

For special occasions perhaps zabaglione, ice cream or water ice, together with a cake or almond/honey cakes bought from the local pastry shop, may be served. For the most part, Italians prefer to visit the coffee houses to sample ice cream, cakes and chocolates. The variety is enormous, the temptation irresistible!

Italian cooking does not depend on the use of expensive ingredients, skilful processes or ornate presentation, but rather on its simplicity. This makes it equally suitable for inexperienced cooks and experts who wish to add variety of style, flavour and colour to their repertoire. So whether it be a simple family meal or a dinner party for friends, try cooking 'Italian style'. Buon appetito!

Ingredients You Will Need

Many of the ingredients you will need for the recipes in this book are probably already in your kitchen cupboard. If, however, you intend to cook 'Italian style' on a regular basis, it is worth stocking up by finding the best sources of ingredients you would expect in an Italian kitchen.

Fresh vegetables, salads and fruit Buy good quality and in small quantities to make sure that they are fresh, crisp and colourful. Remember that many Italian women shop daily in their local market to ensure that they are getting the best quality!

Pasta Pasta is a mixture of durum wheat flour, salt, egg, olive oil and hot water and is traditionally made in many Italian homes. Once the technique of getting the dough to exactly the right consistency, and rolling and stretching the dough paper thin is mastered, many Italian cooks would never consider cooking the packet varieties. However, it requires patience, time and space. Fresh pasta is sold in some delicatessens, otherwise rely on the wide selection of packet varieties that are now on sale in local supermarkets. Available types include spaghetti, tagliatelle, macaroni, lasagne, cannelloni (usually stuffed and rolled), ravioli (stuffed packets of pasta) and a variety of twists, letters and stars which add interest and shape to composite dishes.

Rice Arborio or Piedmontese rice is the usual choice for risotto. If it is not possible to purchase Italian rice, short-grain rice will give the characteristic creamy consistency.

Pulses The most frequently used are canelli, bortelli, kidney beans, chickpeas and lentils. These can all be bought in dried form, soaked overnight and cooked very thoroughly. Most varieties are now also available in cans.

Polenta Polenta is made from yellow corn meal. It is mixed with water and salt and cooked until thick. It is usually served with butter or ragu sauce and grated Parmesan cheese.

Cheeses Every region of Italy produces its own variety of cheese. However, many of these do not travel well and are therefore not exported. Those that you are likely to find in a delicatessen are:

Parmesan A very hard, pungent cheese that is usually very finely grated. It stores almost indefinitely. Pecorino cheese is used in the same way, but has a different flavour.

Bel Paese A soft, creamy cheese with a delicate flavour. It melts and can be used in cooking.

Mozzarella Originally made with buffalo's milk. A mild, soft cheese which can be eaten fresh or used in cooking.

Gorgonzola A strong, blue-veined cheese. It was first produced in northern Italy in the 9th century.

Dolcelatte A mild, creamy, blue-veined cheese.

Ricotta A smooth, white, bland cheese that can be used in main dishes or desserts. If you have difficulty buying this cheese you can use cream cheese, or cottage cheese mashed with a little cream, instead.

Fontina A fat, rich, slightly soft cheese which melts very well.

Herbs Much used in Italian cookery. If possible grow your own, or buy fresh. The most frequently used varieties are parsley (flat-leaved type), basil, oregano, marjoram, rosemary, bay leaf, borage and fennel.

Garlic Keep a supply of fresh garlic, and perhaps some garlic powder or paste.

Spices Frequently used in sweet dishes – nutmeg, cinnamon, cloves, aniseed, vanilla pods.

Olives There is a large range of sizes both green and black. Store in a jar topped up with olive oil.

Olive oil Comes in different grades which indicate quality. Buy the best quality you can afford.

Capers Pickled green flower buds – an essential ingredient of Mediterranean cooking.

Vinegar Use red or white wine vinegar.

Nuts Almonds, hazelnuts and pine kernels are frequently used in Italian cooking.

Honey Often used as a sweetener.

SOUPS & STARTERS

Tomato Soup

PREPARATION TIME: 15 minutes

COOKING TIME: 45 minutes

SERVES: 4 people

120g/4oz short-cut/elbow macaroni
30g/1oz butter or margarine
1 small onion, peeled and chopped
1 small green pepper, cored, seeds
  removed, and chopped
15g/½oz flour
1 litre/2 pints brown stock, or water
  plus 2 beef stock cubes
460g/1lb tomatoes, chopped
2 tbsps tomato purée
1 tbsp grated horseradish
Salt and pepper

GARNISH
2 tbsps soured cream
1 tbsp chopped parsley

Heat the butter in a pan. Cover and cook the onion and green pepper for 5 minutes. Add the flour and stir. Add stock, tomatoes and tomato purée. Simmer for 15 minutes. Purée the soup and pass though a sieve. Return to the pan, and season with salt and pepper to taste. Add the macaroni 10 minutes before serving. Simmer and stir occasionally. Add the horseradish before serving. Garnish with soured cream and parsley. Serve immediately.

Bean Soup

PREPARATION TIME: 15 minutes

COOKING TIME: 1 hour 45 minutes

SERVES: 4 people

430g/15oz tin kidney beans

60g/2oz bacon, rind removed, and chopped
1 stick celery, chopped
1 small onion, peeled and chopped
1 clove garlic, crushed
90g/3oz tin plum tomatoes, chopped
  and seeds removed
1 litre/2 pints water
1 chicken stock cube
1 tbsp chopped parsley
1 tsp basil
120g/4oz wholemeal ring pasta
Salt and pepper

Place the kidney beans, bacon, celery, onion, garlic, parsley, basil, tomatoes and water in a large pan. Bring to the boil and add stock cube and salt and pepper to taste. Cover and cook over a low heat for about 1½ hours. Raise heat and add the pasta, stirring well. Stir frequently until pasta is cooked but still firm – about 10 minutes. Serve immediately.

Above: Bean Soup (top) and Tomato Soup (bottom).

Minestra

PREPARATION TIME: 15 minutes	
COOKING TIME: 45 minutes	
SERVES: 4 people	

120g/4oz short-cut/elbow macaroni
30ml/2 tbsps olive oil
1 onion
1 carrot
1 stick celery
1¹/₂ litres/3 pints water
225g/8oz fresh spinach
2 tomatoes
1 tsp rosemary
2 tbsps chopped parsley
2 cloves garlic, crushed
60g/2oz Parmesan cheese, grated
Salt and pepper

Cut the onion, carrot and celery into thick matchstick strips. Heat the oil in a large, heavy pan, and fry the vegetable strips until just browning, stirring occasionally. Pour on the water, add salt and pepper and simmer for 20 minutes. Meanwhile, wash and cut spinach leaves into shreds, add to soup and cook for 10 minutes. Scald and skin the tomatoes, and chop roughly, removing seeds. Add the tomatoes, macaroni, garlic, parsley and rosemary to the soup, and simmer a further 10 minutes. Adjust seasoning. Serve with grated Parmesan cheese if desired.

Meatball Soup

PREPARATION TIME: 10 minutes	
COOKING TIME: 1 hour 40 minutes	
OVEN: 180°C/350°F/Gas Mark 3	
SERVES: 4 people	

225g/8oz minced beef
60g/2oz breadcrumbs
1 egg, beaten
460g/1lb beef bones
1 stick celery
1 carrot
1 onion
15ml/1 tbsp oil
400g/14oz tin plum tomatoes
175g/6oz soup pastà
1 tbsp chopped parsley

Salt and pepper

Place the bones, peeled carrot, onion and celery in a large saucepan and cover with cold water. Bring to the boil: cover and simmer for one hour at least. Meanwhile, mix together lightly the beaten egg with minced beef, breadcrumbs and plenty of seasoning. Roll a teaspoon amount into small balls and place on a roasting tin with the oil. Bake in a preheated oven for 45 minutes, turning occasionally. Strain stock into a saucepan. Push tomatoes and their juice through sieve, and add to the stock. Bring to the boil, and simmer for 15 minutes. Add pasta and cook for 10 minutes, stirring frequently. Add meatballs, adjust seasoning, and stir in the chopped parsley. Serve hot.

Chickpea Soup

PREPARATION TIME: Chickpeas soaked overnight, plus 5 minutes	
COOKING TIME: 1 hour 20 minutes	
SERVES: 4 people	

140g/5oz dried chickpeas
120g/4oz soup pasta
2 cloves garlic
45ml/3 tbsps olive oil
1 tsp basil
400g/14oz tin plum tomatoes, chopped
1 litre/1³/₄ pints water
1 chicken stock cube
2 tbsps Parmesan cheese, grated
Salt and pepper

Soak the chickpeas overnight in enough water to cover by 25mm/1 inch. Discard the water in which the chickpeas have soaked. Place the chickpeas in a large, heavy pan, and cover with 25mm/1 inch of water. Bring to the boil and simmer, covered, for about 1 hour until chickpeas are tender, ensuring that they do not boil dry. Heat the olive oil in a heavy pan, and sauté garlic cloves. When browned, remove and discard garlic cloves. Add the tomatoes and their juice, water and basil, and cook together for 20 minutes. Add the drained chickpeas, crumbled stock cube and salt and pepper to taste. Stir well; simmer for a further 10 minutes. Bring back to the boil. Add the pasta, and cook, stirring frequently, for 10 minutes. Mix in half of the Parmesan cheese. Adjust seasoning and serve immediately, with remaining Parmesan cheese sprinkled on top. *Note:* Soup may be puréed before pasta is added, if desired.

Mussel Soup

PREPARATION TIME: 15 minutes	
COOKING TIME: 20 minutes	
SERVES: 4 people	

2¹/₄ pints live mussels, scrubbed clean
2 tbsps butter or margarine
2 cloves garlic, crushed
2 onions, peeled and chopped
280ml/¹/₂ pint dry white wine
2 tbsps chopped parsley
2 tbsps lemon juice
Salt
Pepper

GARNISH
Chopped parsley

Place the mussels, butter, garlic, onions, wine, parsley and a pinch of freshly ground black pepper in a pan, and cover. Place over a high heat and cook for a few minutes. Shake the pan to move the mussels and distribute the heat well. When mussels have all opened, transfer to a serving dish and keep warm. Discard any that remain closed. Strain juices and return to the pan. Reduce liquid by half over a high heat. Adjust seasoning. Whisk in the lemon juice and pour hot soup over mussels. Serve immediately, sprinkled with chopped parsley.

Facing page: Minestra (top), Meatball Soup (centre right) and Chickpea Soup (bottom).

Minestrone

| PREPARATION TIME: 30 minutes |
| COOKING TIME: 1 hour 15 minutes |
| SERVES: 4 people |

1 carrot, cut into strips
1 leek, sliced
1 turnip, cut into strips
3 tomatoes, skinned and diced
1 stick celery, chopped
4 slices bacon, blanched and diced
1/4 small cabbage, sliced
3 cloves garlic, crushed
1 onion, peeled and sliced
2 tbsps butter or margarine
1 litre/1 3/4 pints good, fat-free chicken stock
60g/2oz short-cut/elbow macaroni
Salt
Pepper

ACCOMPANIMENT
Freshly grated Parmesan cheese, if desired

Melt the butter in a pan and add the garlic, onion, leek and celery. Cover and cook over a gentle heat for 15 minutes without colouring. Add the carrot and turnip, stock and salt and pepper to taste. Bring to the boil, cover and simmer for 30 minutes. Add the cabbage and simmer for a further 5 minutes. Add the tomato and macaroni and simmer gently, uncovered, for 15 minutes. Meanwhile, grill the bacon until crisp. Serve on top of the soup with a side serving of Parmesan cheese if desired.

Fish Soup

| PREPARATION TIME: 15 minutes |
| COOKING TIME: 40 minutes |
| SERVES: 4 people |

900g/2lbs of bass, whiting, monkfish
    and/or bream, skin and bones
    removed, cut into bite-size pieces
2 onions, peeled and chopped
3 cloves garlic, crushed
2 tomatoes, skinned and chopped
1 tbsp oil
Sprig of fresh thyme
1 bay leaf

2 pieces thinly pared orange rind
150ml/5 fl oz dry white wine
Salt and pepper

GARNISH
Chopped parsley

Make a stock with the heads and trimmings of the fish, one-third of the onion and 1 litre/1 3/4 pints of water. Simmer for 15 minutes, then strain. Put the oil in a heavy pan and heat gently. Add the garlic and remaining onion. Cover and fry gently for 5 minutes without colouring. Add the fish, tomatoes, herbs, orange rind, wine, salt and pepper and stock. Bring to the boil and simmer for 10 minutes. Remove the bay leaf, thyme and orange rind. Serve hot, sprinkled with parsley.

This page: Mussel Soup. Facing page: Minestrone.

Lobster Cream Soup

PREPARATION TIME: 20 minutes

COOKING TIME: 1 hour

SERVES: 4 people

1 cooked lobster
1 onion, peeled and diced
1 stick celery, cut into 2.5cm/1-inch slices
1 carrot, diced
1 litre/1³/4 pints fish stock or water
1 bay leaf
6 peppercorns
Parsley stalks
Salt
Pepper
2 tbsps butter or margarine
2 tbsps flour
1 tsp lemon juice
2 tbsps cream
3 tbsps white wine
2 tsps tomato purée

GARNISH
Cream and chopped parsley

Remove meat from the body, tail and claws of the lobster. Put the lobster shell, stock or water, onion, carrot, celery, herbs and seasoning into a pan. Bring to the boil and simmer for 45 minutes. Allow to cool. Strain and reserve the stock. Meanwhile, cut the lobster meat into bite-size pieces. Melt the butter in the pan, stir in the flour, and cook for 1 minute. Remove from the heat and stir in the reserved stock gradually. Return to the heat. Bring to the boil and simmer for 5 minutes, stirring continuously. Remove from the heat and add the lemon juice, tomato purée, wine and cream and whisk in well. Adjust seasoning. Add the lobster meat and garnish with cream and chopped parsley if desired. Serve immediately.

Beef and Pepper Soup

PREPARATION TIME: 20 minutes

COOKING TIME: 2 hours 45 minutes

SERVES: 4 people

680g/1¹/2 lbs skirt or chuck steak, cut into 2.5cm/1-inch cubes
4 medium onions, peeled and chopped roughly or quartered
1 green pepper, cored, seeds removed, and chopped
4 tomatoes, skinned and quartered
4 tbsps tomato purée
570ml/1 pint good beef stock
2 tbsps butter or margarine
1 tbsp oil
460g/1lb potatoes, peeled and cut into bite-size pieces
1 tbsp flour
Salt and pepper

Heat the oil in a pan. When hot, add the steak in batches so as not to overcrowd, and sauté over a high heat until well browned all over. Remove and set aide. Add the butter, onion and green pepper, and fry until the onion is lightly browned. Stir in the flour. Remove from the heat. Add the stock, return to the heat and bring to the boil, stirring continuously. Add the tomato, tomato purée, and salt and pepper to taste. Reduce the heat, return the meat, cover and simmer for 2 hours, stirring occasionally and adding more stock or water if necessary. Add the potatoes and cook gently for a further 20 minutes, or until the potatoes are cooked through.

Vegetable and Lentil Soup

PREPARATION TIME: 30 minutes

COOKING TIME: 1 hour 45 minutes

SERVES: 4 people

1 litre/1³/4 pints good beef stock
460g/1lb spinach, stalks removed, and shredded
2 onions, peeled and diced
2 carrots, scraped and diced
2 potatoes, peeled and diced
3 sticks celery, sliced
1 tbsp chopped parsley
2 tbsps tomato purée
¹/2 cup lentils
Salt
Pepper

This page: Beef and Pepper Soup.
Facing page: Fish Soup (top) and
Lobster Cream Soup (bottom).

Heat the stock in a pan. When hot, add the vegetables, parsley, tomato purée and seasoning. Bring to the boil and simmer for 1 hour. Add the lentils and simmer for a further 30 minutes, stirring occasionally. Adjust seasoning if necessary. Serve hot.

Vegetable Soup

PREPARATION TIME: 20 minutes

COOKING TIME: 50 minutes

SERVES: 4 people

2 medium onions, peeled and finely chopped
1 carrot, finely diced
½ small turnip, finely diced
800ml/1½ pints beef stock
2 tbsps butter or margarine
1 leek, cut into small rings
1 tbsp tomato purée
2 tbsps chopped parsley
Salt
Pepper

GARNISH
Chopped parsley

Melt the butter in a saucepan and add the onions. Cook gently over a low heat for 5 minutes or until transparent. Add the carrot and turnip, stock, seasoning and parsley. Bring to the boil and simmer gently for 15 minutes. Add the leek and tomato purée and simmer for a further 20 minutes. Garnish with chopped parsley. Serve hot.

Red Pepper Soup

PREPARATION TIME: 15 minutes

COOKING TIME: 45 minutes

SERVES: 4 people

1 medium onion, peeled and finely chopped
3 tomatoes
3 red peppers
2 tbsps butter or margarine
1 litre/1¾ pints chicken stock
Salt
Pepper

GARNISH
Chopped parsley and sliced red pepper

Remove the core and seeds from the peppers. Slice a pepper for garnish and set aside. Chop the remaining peppers and tomatoes into small pieces. Melt the butter in a large saucepan and add the onion, tomatoes and peppers and fry gently for 5 minutes, stirring continuously. Pour on the chicken stock, add salt and pepper and bring to the boil. Simmer for 30 minutes. Push the soup through a strainer to remove the skin and any seeds. Adjust the seasoning. Add a pinch of sugar if desired. Serve hot or cold, sprinkled with parsley and garnished with a slice of red pepper.

Broccoli Timbales

PREPARATION TIME: 10 minutes

COOKING TIME: 30 minutes

OVEN TEMPERATURE:
190°C/375°F/Gas Mark 5

SERVES: 4 people

4 broccoli florets
2 tbsps butter or margarine
2 tbsps flour
1 tsp ground nutmeg
280ml/½ pint milk
2 eggs, beaten
Salt and pepper

This page: Vegetable Soup. Facing page: Red Pepper Soup (top) and Vegetable and Lentil Soup (bottom).

Blanch the broccoli in boiled salted water for 3 minutes. Drain and refresh under cold water. Drain and set aside. Melt the butter in a saucepan. Stir in the flour and nutmeg and cook for 1 minute. Remove from the heat and stir in the milk gradually. Return to heat and bring to the boil, stirring continuously. Cook for 3 minutes. Add salt and white pepper to taste and beat well. Set aside to cool. Butter 4 ramekins. Place a floret of broccoli in each one with the stem pointing upwards. Beat the eggs into the cooled white sauce and pour into each ramekin. Place in a shallow baking tin. Pour boiling water into the tin to a depth of 2.5cm/1 inch. Bake in a preheated oven for 15 minutes, or until just setting. Remove from the oven and turn out onto individual plates. Serve immediately.

Onion-Egg-Tomato Bake

PREPARATION TIME: 15 minutes

COOKING TIME: 20 minutes

OVEN TEMPERATURE: 200°C/ 400°F/Gas Mark 6

SERVES: 4 people

60g/2oz butter or margarine
2 medium onions, sliced
2 tbsps flour
150ml/5 fl oz milk
Salt and pepper
4 eggs, hard-boiled
2 tomatoes, skinned and thinly sliced
1 tbsp breadcrumbs
1 tbsp freshly grated Parmesan cheese

GARNISH
Parsley

Melt the butter in a pan. Add the onions and fry over a gentle heat until softened but not coloured. Remove with a slotted spoon and set aside. Stir in the flour and cook for 1 minute. Remove from the heat and gradually stir in the milk. Beat well and return to the heat. Cook for 3 minutes, stirring continuously. Add the onions and plenty of salt and pepper. Cut the eggs in half. Remove the yolks and set aside. Rinse and slice the egg whites. Place in the bottom of an ovenproof dish. Cover with the onion mixture, then with a layer of sliced tomatoes. Mix together the egg yolk, breadcrumbs and the Parmesan cheese. Sprinkle mixture over the top and place in an oven until golden. Garnish with parsley.

Mussels alla Genovese

PREPARATION TIME: 15 minutes

COOKING TIME: 5-8 minutes

SERVES: 4 people

1 litre/2 pints mussels
Lemon juice
1 shallot, finely chopped
1 handful fresh basil leaves
1 small bunch parsley
30g/1oz walnut halves
1 clove garlic
2 tbsps freshly grated Parmesan cheese
3-6 tbsps olive oil
2 tbsps butter
Salt and pepper
Flour or oatmeal

GARNISH
Fresh bay leaves or basil leaves

Scrub the mussels well and discard any with broken shells. Put the mussels into a bowl of clean water with a handful of flour or oatmeal. Leave for 1/2 hour, then rinse under clear water. Chop the shallot finely and put into a large saucepan with the lemon juice. Cook until the shallot softens. Add the mussels and a pinch of salt and pepper. Cover the pan and cook the mussels quickly, shaking the pan. When the mussel shells have opened, take them out of the pan, set aside and keep warm. Strain the cooking liquid for possible use later. To prepare Genovese sauce, wash the basil leaves and parsley, peel the garlic clove and chop roughly, and chop the walnuts roughly. Put the herbs, garlic, nuts, 1 tbsp grated cheese and salt and pepper into a food processor and chop roughly. Add the butter and work again. Turn the machine on and add the oil gradually through the feed tube. If the sauce is still too thick, add the reserved liquid from cooking the mussels. Remove top shells from mussels and discard. Arrange mussels evenly in 4 shallow dishes, spoon some of the sauce into each, and sprinkle the top lightly with the remaining Parmesan cheese. Garnish with the bay or basil leaves and serve.

Onion-Egg-Tomato Bake (right) and Broccoli Timbales (below).

Melon Balls in Mulled Wine

PREPARATION TIME: 1 hour

COOKING TIME: 10 minutes

SERVES: 4 people

1 melon
½ bottle red wine
2 cinnamon sticks
4 cloves
3 blades mace
Juice and pared rind of 1 orange
1 tsp freshly grated nutmeg
4 tbsps sugar

Put the wine, orange juice and rind, spices and sugar into a pan and heat gently. Do not allow to boil. When hot, remove from the heat and leave to infuse for an hour. Strain. Meanwhile, cut the melon in half and scrape out seeds. Then make melon balls with a melon-ball scoop, or cut into chunks. Place in individual serving dishes and pour over mulled wine.

Orange, Grapefruit and Mint Salad

PREPARATION TIME: 20 minutes, plus chilling time

SERVES: 4 people

2 grapefruit
3 oranges
1 tbsp sugar
4 sprigs of mint

GARNISH
Mint sprig

Cut the peel and pith off the grapefruit and oranges. Cut carefully inside the skin of each segment to remove each section of flesh. When the skin only is left, squeeze to extract juice over a pan. Repeat with all the fruit. Add the sugar to the pan and set over a gentle heat until the sugar dissolves. Cool. Meanwhile, arrange the orange and grapefruit segments alternately in a dish. Chop mint finely and add to the fruit syrup. Carefully spoon the syrup over the fruit. Chill. Garnish with a sprig of mint.

Fanned Avocado Salad with Prawn and Tomato Dressing

PREPARATION TIME: 20 minutes

SERVES: 4 people

3 tbsps mayonnaise
1 tbsp tomato purée
1 tbsp single cream
Salt and pepper
2 ripe avocados
225g/8oz prawns, shelled and de-veined
Juice of ½ lemon or 1 lime

GARNISH
Lettuce leaves
Lemon or lime slices

Mix together the mayonnaise, tomato purée, cream, and salt and pepper to taste. Mix the prawns with 2 tbsps of the mayonnaise mixture and set aside. Cut the avocados in half. Remove the stones and peel back and remove the skin. Slice down through the flesh 5 or 6 times, keeping the thin end intact. Place on lettuce leaves on serving dishes and press down so that the avocado fans out. Sprinkle over the lemon or lime juice to prevent the flesh from browning. Place the prawns at the side of the dish, around the avocado. Garnish with lemon or lime slices.

This page: Mussels alla Genovese. Facing page: Melon Balls in Mulled Wine (top) and Orange, Grapefruit and Mint Salad (bottom).

Garlic Fried Scallops

PREPARATION TIME: 10 minutes

COOKING TIME: 6-8 minutes

SERVES: 4 people

16 scallops
1 large clove garlic, peeled and chopped
*   finely*
60-90g/2-3oz butter
3 tbsps chopped parsley
2 lemons
Seasoned flour

Rinse the scallops and remove black veins. If scallops are large, cut in half horizontally. Squeeze the juice from 1 lemon. Sprinkle scallops lightly with seasoned flour. Heat the butter in a frying pan and add the chopped garlic and scallops. Fry until pale golden brown. Pour over the lemon juice, and cook to reduce the amount of liquid. Toss in the chopped parsley. Pile the scallops into individual scallop shells or porcelain baking dishes. Keep warm and garnish with lemon wedges before serving.

Chicken Tongue Rolls

PREPARATION TIME: 15 minutes

COOKING TIME: 20 minutes

SERVES: 4 people

4 chicken legs
4 slices of smoked tongue
2 tbsps grated Parmesan cheese
1 tbsp grated fontina cheese
1 tbsp chopped parsley
1 tbsp oil
Salt
Pepper

GARNISH
Parsley
Tomato

Remove bone carefully from the chicken leg, keeping the meat in one piece. Flatten out, and divide the tongue equally between each piece. Mix together the grated cheese, parsley and salt and pepper to taste. Place 1 tbsp of the mixture on each piece of chicken. Roll up the chicken and tie each with string, 2 or 3 times.

Heat the oil in a pan and fry the chicken rolls gently for about 20 minutes, turning occasionally to cook evenly. Remove from the heat and allow to cool. Cut off the string and remove gently. Slice into rounds and serve garnished with parsley and tomato.

Stuffed Mushrooms

PREPARATION TIME: 15 minutes

COOKING TIME: 20 minutes

OVEN TEMPERATURE:
200°C/400°F/Gas Mark 6

SERVES: 4 people

4 large or 8 medium mushrooms, stalks
*   removed*
1 tbsp olive oil
2 medium onions, peeled and chopped
*   finely*
225g/8oz spinach, trimmed, cooked and
*   chopped finely*
2 tbsps fresh white breadcrumbs
4 tbsps butter or margarine
4 cloves garlic, crushed
1 egg, beaten
1/2 tsp nutmeg
Salt
Pepper

GARNISH
1 tbsp chopped parsley

Heat the butter in a pan. Add the garlic, onion and nutmeg and fry gently until the onion has softened. Remove from the pan and set aside to cool. Meanwhile, heat the oil in a pan and sauté the mushrooms on both sides until lightly browned. Place underside-up in a shallow ovenproof dish. Mix together the onion mixture, spinach, breadcrumbs and salt and freshly ground black pepper to taste. Stir in the beaten egg. Cover each mushroom cap with the mixture, shaping neatly. Cover with aluminium foil and bake in a hot oven for 10 minutes. Serve immediately, garnished with chopped parsley.

This page: Chicken Tongue Rolls.
Facing page: Stuffed Mushrooms (top) and Fanned Avocado Salad with Prawn and Tomato Dressing (bottom).

Sole Surprise

PREPARATION TIME: 30 minutes	
COOKING TIME: 30 minutes	
OVEN TEMPERATURE: 220°C/425°F/Gas Mark 7	
SERVES: 4 people	

This consists of little puff pastry 'boxes' filled with spinach, with the fillets of sole laid on top and coated with a cheese sauce. It makes an interesting luncheon or starter for four people.

4 small or 2 large fillets of sole
225g/8oz frozen puff pastry
225g/8oz frozen spinach
4 tbsps butter

SAUCE
2 tbsps butter
2 tbsps flour
300ml/¹/₂ pint milk
Pinch fennel
Salt and pepper
60g/2oz grated cheese

Roll out the defrosted pastry into a rectangle 13x20cm/5x8 inches. Cut it

down the centre in both directions to make four rectangles 6.5x10cm/2¹/₂x4 inches. Carry out the following procedure with each one. Fold over, short sides together. Cut out the centre with a sharp knife, leaving 1.25cm/¹/₂-inch all round. Roll out the centre piece on a floured board until it is the same size as the 1.25cm/¹/₂-inch "frame". Brush the edges with

This page: Scallops au Gratin (top) and Sole Surprise (bottom). Facing page: Garlic Fried Scallops (top) and Scampi and Avacado Cocktail (bottom).

milk and put the "frame" on the base. Brush the top with milk and put it on a greased baking sheet. Bake them in the oven for 10-15 minutes. Meanwhile, put the spinach in a pan with 6mm/¼-inch water and a little salt. Cover and cook for 4-5 minutes. Drain and beat in half the butter. Skin the fillets and, if necessary, cut them in two. Use the rest of the butter to coat two plates and put the fillets on one and cover them with the other. Cook them over a pan of boiling water for twenty minutes. For the sauce, melt the 2 tbsps butter with the flour to make a roux. Gradually stir in the milk. Bring to the boil. Reduce the heat and add the fennel and salt and pepper; cook for another minute or two. Remove from the heat and stir in the grated cheese. Divide the spinach between the four boxes. Lay the sole on top and coat with the cheese sauce.

Scampi and Avocado Cocktail

PREPARATION TIME: 20 minutes

SERVES: 4 people

225g/8oz cooked langoustines or large prawns
2 oranges
2 large, ripe avocados
1 small red onion or 2 spring onions
60g/2oz double cream
2 tbsps tomato purée
2 tbsps mayonnaise
2 tsps lemon juice
12 (approx) black olives, stoned and sliced
Pinch of Cayenne pepper
Pinch sugar
Salt
Freshly ground pepper
Lettuce

Peel the oranges over a bowl to reserve the juice. Peel the cooked scampi and set aside. To prepare the dressing, whip the cream until thick, and mix with the tomato purée, mayonnaise, lemon juice, Cayenne pepper, sugar, salt and pepper and some of the reserved orange juice to thin down to the proper consistency –

the dressing should be slightly thick. Chop the onion finely. Cut the avocados in half lengthways and take out the stones. Peel carefully and cut each half into 4-6 long slices. Shred the lettuce and put onto serving dishes. Arrange the avocado slices in a fan shape on top of the lettuce. Brush each side lightly with the orange juice to keep green. Arrange an orange segment in between each slice. Pile the scampi up at the top of the avocado fan and coat with some of the dressing. Garnish with olives and sprinkle over chopped onion.

Pepper Appetizer

PREPARATION TIME: 15 minutes

COOKING TIME: 1 hour 15 minutes

SERVES: 4 people

1 green pepper
1 red pepper
2 tomatoes
2 onions
60ml/4 tbsps white vinegar
2 tbps oil
Salt

Remove core and seeds from the peppers and slice lengthways. Peel and slice the onions and tomatoes. Heat the oil in a large saucepan. Add the vegetables and salt to taste and simmer, covered, for 1 hour, stirring occasionally. Remove the lid, add the vinegar and simmer for a further 15 minutes. Allow to cool and chill in the refrigerator.

Aubergine Appetizer

PREPARATION TIME: 15 minute

COOKING TIME: 20 minutes

SERVES: 4 people

1 large aubergine
4 tbsps oil
2 cloves garlic, crushed
2 ripe tomatoes, peeled, seeds removed, and chopped
1 tbsp tomato purée
4 tbsps water
Salt and pepper

Cut the aubergine lengthways into 1x6cm/¼x2½-inch strips. Heat the oil in a pan until hot. Add the aubergine and cook for 5 minutes or until cooked. Remove from the pan with a slotted spoon. Add extra oil as necessary and heat. Fry the garlic for 30 seconds. Add the tomatoes, tomato purée, salt and pepper, and water and cook for 10 minutes, or until the sauce is thick. Add the aubergine and stir together. Adjust seasoning and cook for a further 5 minutes. Serve hot or cold.

Scallops au Gratin

PREPARATION TIME: 10 minutes

COOKING TIME: 15 minutes

SERVES: 4 people

2 tbsps oil
60g/2oz butter
2-3 tbsps finely chopped shallots
1 wineglass of white wine
4 scallops
2 tbsps double cream
2 egg yolks
30g/1oz grated Parmesan cheese
4 tbsps white breadcrumbs

Heat the oil and butter in a heavy frying pan. Add the shallots and cook gently until they soften. Slice the white parts of the scallops. Increase the heat, stir in the white wine and then the sliced scallops and cook fairly briskly for 2-3 minutes. Slice the coral of the scallops and add to the pan, cooking the mixture for a further minute. Add the cream to the lightly beaten egg yolks. Stir gently over a low heat until the mixture thickens, adding a sprinkling of salt and pepper. Divide between four scallop shells, making sure each one has its fair share of the coral. Sprinkle 1 tbsp of cheese and 1 tbsp of breadcrumbs on each and place under a preheated grill until just beginning to brown on top. Serve immediately with brown bread.

Facing page: Pepper Appetizer (top) and Aubergine Appetizer (bottom).

Cheese Puffs

PREPARATION TIME: 20 minutes
COOKING TIME: 20 minutes
SERVES: 4 people

PASTRY
120g/4 oz flour
Pinch of salt
90g/3oz butter or margarine
225ml/8 fl oz water
3 medium eggs, lightly beaten

FILLING
60g/2 oz fontina cheese, grated
60g/2oz Parmesan cheese, grated
1 egg, beaten
1 egg yolk, beaten, for glaze

Preheat oven to 190°C/375°F/Gas Mark 5. Sift the flour and salt onto a sheet of greaseproof paper. Place the butter and water in a pan over a gentle heat. When the butter has melted, bring to the boil and immediately add all the flour. Beat well until the mixture is smooth. Leave to cool. Add the eggs gradually to the mixture, beating well. Using a teaspoon or a piping bag with a plain tube, shape the mixture into balls about the size of golf balls onto a lightly greased baking sheet. Place in the oven and increase the heat to 200°C/400°F/Gas Mark 6. Bake for 10 minutes until firm on the outside. Remove from the oven and make a hole in the bottom or side. Mix together the cheese and egg. Pipe in the cheese mixture and brush the tops with egg yolk. Return to the oven for 5 minutes. Serve immediately.

Anchovy Pâté with Crudités

PREPARATION TIME: 15 minutes
SERVES: 4 people

225g/8oz tin anchovy fillets in olive oil
70ml/2 fl oz olive oil
60g/2oz curd cheese
120g/4oz pitted black olives
60g/2oz capers
1 tbsp Dijon mustard

1 tsp ground pepper

Put all the ingredients into the bowl of a liquidiser or food processor and run the machine until well mixed. The mixture may have to be worked in 2 batches. Serve with French bread or toast, and raw vegetables of all kinds – tomatoes, mushrooms, celery, radishes, French beans, cauliflower, carrots, cucumber, peppers, spring onions, or quarters of hard-boiled eggs.

This page: **Tomato and Pepper Ice.**
Facing page: **Anchovy Pâté with Crudités.**

in a freezer for 30 minutes or until half-frozen. Meanwhile, remove core and seeds from the peppers and dice finely. Remove tomato ice from the freezer and transfer to a bowl, breaking up with the back of a fork. Mix in peppers. Re-freeze for a further 2 hours, stirring occasionally. For a garnish, make tomato flowers. Peel the tomatoes (drop into boiling water, count to ten slowly, then rinse in cold water, remove skins). Starting at one end, with a sharp knife slice a continuous strip around the tomato. Form into a rose shape. Serve on top of the tomato and pepper ice.

Stuffed Eggs

PREPARATION TIME: 20 minutes	
COOKING TIME: 15 minutes	
SERVES: 4 people	

6 medium eggs
1 tbsp vinegar
1 small tin of pink salmon
Paprika
2 tbsps peas
4-5 mushrooms
225g/8oz cream cheese
Salt and pepper

GARNISH
Stuffed olive
Red pepper or tomato
Black olive

Put the eggs into a saucepan of gently boiling water with 1 tbsp of vinegar and boil gently for 12 minutes. Remove and rinse immediately in cold water. Remove the shells carefully and keep the eggs in cold water until ready to use. Cut the boiled eggs in half and carefully remove the yolks. Rinse the whites. Push the yolks through a sieve and put aside for the fillings. Soften the cream cheese by beating. Drain and flake the salmon. Mix carefully with ¹/₃ of the cream cheese. Add a pinch of paprika and salt and pepper to taste. Pipe or spoon the filling into 4 egg white halves. Garnish with half a stuffed olive. Wash and trim the

Tomato and Pepper Ice

PREPARATION TIME: 15 minutes, plus freezing time	
SERVES: 4 people	

115ml/4 fl oz tomato juice
Juice of 1 lemon
6 ice cubes
¹/₂ small green pepper
¹/₂ small red pepper

GARNISH
4 tomato flowers

Crush ice. Put the tomato juice, lemon juice and ice in blender. Blend together. Put into ice trays and place mushrooms. Chop very finely and add to 1/3 of the cream cheese. Add salt or pepper to taste. Pipe or spoon the filling into 4 egg white halves. Garnish with red pepper or tomato. Cook the peas until tender. Push through a strainer. Add the yolks of the eggs and 1/3 of the cream cheese. Pipe or spoon the filling into the remaining 4 egg white halves and garnish with a slice of black olive.

Gorgonzola Tarts

PREPARATION TIME: 30 minutes

COOKING TIME: 20 minutes

OVEN TEMPERATURE: 190°C/375°F/Gas Mark 5

SERVES: 4 people

PASTRY
175g/6oz flour
Pinch of salt
90g/3oz butter or margarine
2 tbsps lard
Cold water

FILLING
120g 4oz Gorgonzola cheese
120g/4oz cream cheese
2 tbsps single cream
2 eggs, lightly beaten

Sift the salt and flour into a bowl. Cut the cold fat into small pieces and drop into the flour. Cut fat into the flour. When well cut in, use fingers to rub in completely. Mix to a firm but pliable dough with cold water. Knead on a lightly floured board until smooth. Chill for 15 minutes in the refrigerator. Meanwhile, gently melt together the Gorgonzola cheese and cream cheese in a pan, stirring continuously. When melted, set aside to cool. Mix together the cream and beaten eggs, and add to the cheese mixture, stirring well. Roll out the dough on a lightly floured board. Using a 75mm/3-inch fluted pastry-cutter, cut out rounds of pastry. Line a patty tin. Prick the bottom of the pastry shells with a fork. Spoon the mixture into individual pastry shells and bake in the oven for about 15 minutes until golden brown.

This page: Stuffed Eggs. Facing page: Gorgonzola Tarts (top) and Cheese Puffs (bottom).

SALADS & VEGETABLE DISHES

Salad of Pasta Quills

PREPARATION TIME: 15 minutes

COOKING TIME: 15 minutes

SERVES: 4 people

225g/8oz cups penne
3 tomatoes, quartered
120g/4oz green beans, cooked
½ cucumber, cut into batons
1 x 200g/7oz tin tuna fish, drained
  and flaked
12 black olives, halved, with stones
  removed
6-8 anchovy fillets, drained, and
  soaked in milk if desired
120ml/4 fl oz French dressing

Cook the penne in lots of boiling
salted water until tender but still firm.
Rinse in cold water; drain, and leave
to dry. Put the flaked tuna in the base
of a salad dish. Toss the pasta together
with the tomatoes, cucumber, green
beans, olives, and anchovies, and
then pour over oil and vinegar
dressing. Mix together well.

Tuna Salad Naples Style

PREPARATION TIME: 20 minutes

COOKING TIME: 15-20 minutes

SERVES: 4 people

1 tin tuna, drained
120g/4oz prawns
6-8 canned anchovy fillets, drained
4 ripe tomatoes
4 hard-boiled eggs
1 red pepper
60g/2oz black olives, pitted
120g/4oz green beans

2 large potatoes, or 6 small new potatoes
2 tbsps white wine vinegar
6 tbsps olive oil
3 tbsps chopped mixed herbs
Salt and pepper

Peel and cook the potatoes until

tender. If using large potatoes, cut
into 1.25cm/½-inch dice (new

**This page: Salad of Pasta Quills. Facing
page: Tuna Salad Naples Style (top) and
Rice and Sole Salad (bottom).**

potatoes may be sliced into 5mm/¼-inch rounds) Trim the beans, put into boiling salted water for about 3-4 minutes, or until just barely cooked. Drain and rinse under cold water, then leave to drain dry. Cut the olives in half lengthways. Cut the anchovies in half lengthways, then through the middle. Cut the tomatoes into quarters (or eighths, if large) and remove the cores. Mix the vinegar and oil together for the vinaigrette dressing, and add the seasoning and chopped herbs. Cut the red pepper into thin shreds. Mix together all the ingredients, including the prawns, and toss in the dressing. Quarter the eggs and toss into the other ingredients very carefully – do not break up the eggs. Pile onto dishes and serve.

Rice and Sole Salad

PREPARATION TIME: 20 minutes
COOKING TIME: 8-10 minutes
OVEN TEMPERATURE:
180°C/350°F/Gas Mark 4
SERVES: 4 people

4 sole fillets, skinned
Slice of onion
Lemon juice
4-6 peppercorns
175g/6oz long-grain rice
1 green pepper
1 red pepper
1 small aubergine
75ml/5 tbsps olive oil
Salt and pepper
1 tbsp chopped mixed herbs
1 shallot, finely chopped
1 clove garlic
280ml/½ pint prepared mayonnaise
1 tsp tomato purée
1 tsp paprika
2 bunches watercress

Put the sole fillets into a baking dish. Add the onion, a squeeze of lemon juice, peppercorns and enough water to cover. Sprinkle with salt, cover with buttered foil, and bake in an oven for about 8-10 minutes. Allow the fish to cool in the liquid, then cut into 2.5cm/1-inch pieces. Cook the rice for 12-15 minutes, or until just tender. Drain under hot water, then cold, and leave to drain completely dry. Chop the green and red peppers into 5mm/¼-inch dice. Cut the aubergine in half lengthways, score each half, sprinkle with salt, and leave to stand for 30 minutes. Rinse the aubergine well, then dry it. Cut it into 1.25cm/½-inch cubes and fry very quickly in 2 tbsps olive oil. Add salt and pepper, and toss with the cooked rice, and red and green pepper. Add a pinch of the chopped herbs. Make a dressing with 1 tbsp lemon juice, the remaining olive oil and the shallot. Toss with the rice. Crush the garlic and work it together with the mayonnaise, tomato purée and paprika. Add salt, pepper and the rest of the chopped herbs. Thin with a little milk or hot water. Adjust seasoning. Arrange the rice salad on one side of each of four serving dishes, and put the sole fillets on the other side. Spoon the mayonnaise dressing over the fillets. Divide the two sides with small bunches of the watercress.

Chicken and Salmon

PREPARATION TIME: 20 minutes
COOKING TIME: 15-20 minutes
OVEN TEMPERATURE:
180°C/350°F/Gas Mark 4
SERVES: 4 people

4 boned chicken breasts
90g/3oz fresh salmon, or canned red salmon
White wine
4 anchovies
120ml/4 fl ozcup olive oil
2 egg yolks
Salt and pepper
1½ tbsps lemon juice
1 tbsp chopped parsley

GARNISH
4 small pickled gherkins
1 tbsp capers
Curly endive

Buy prepared chicken breasts. Put them on a sheet of foil and sprinkle over salt, pepper and a little white wine. Seal foil well. Put into a baking dish and bake in the oven for about 15 minutes, or until cooked through. Open foil packet and allow to cool. Reserve the juice from the chicken. Poach the fresh salmon (or drain tinned salmon) and remove bones. Put the salmon and anchovies into a food processor or blender and work until broken up. Work in the egg yolks, and salt and pepper. With the machine running, add the oil gradually. Add the lemon juice to taste and adjust the seasoning. Stir in the cooking liquid from the chicken to give the sauce the consistency of thin cram; if it is too thick add a few drops of milk or water. Put the cold chicken breasts onto a plate and coat with all the sauce. Before serving, garnish the dish with capers and gherkins. Serve with a green salad or a cold rice salad.

Mussels Marinara (top left) and Chicken and Salmon (left).

Mussels Marinara

| PREPARATION TIME: 15 minutes |
| COOKING TIME: 15 minutes |
| SERVES: 4 people |

2 pints mussels
1 onion, chopped
120ml/4 fl oz white wine
675g/1¹/₂lbs tomatoes
1 clove garlic
Lemon juice
Salt and pepper
Pinch Cayenne pepper
1 chopped shallot
1 tsp fennel seed
1 tsp crushed oregano
1 bay leaf
1 tbsp chopped fresh basil leaves
2 tbsps olive oil

GARNISH
Chopped parsley
Black olives

Scrub the mussels well, discarding any with broken shells. Put into a pan with the chopped onion, white wine, squeeze of lemon juice, salt and pepper. Cover and cook quickly until the mussels open, discarding any that do not. Remove the mussels from the shells and leave to cool. Heat the olive oil in a saucepan and add the crushed garlic and shallot. Cook until just lightly brown. Blend in the tomatoes, herbs and fennel seeds. Add the seasoning and cooking liquid from the mussels and bring to the boil. Allow the sauce to boil rapidly until well reduced. Leave the sauce to cool, then mix with mussels. Serve garnished with the chopped parsley and black olives. Serve with a green salad and Italian bread.

Prawn and Pasta Salad

| PREPARATION TIME: 10 minutes |
| COOKING TIME: 20 minutes |
| SERVES: 4 people |

225g/8oz soup pasta
225g/8oz prawns, shelled and deveined
1 tsp paprika
Juice of ¹/₂ a lemon
1¹/₂ tsps powdered saffron
1 tsp tomato purée
2 tbsps olive oil
1 small onion, peeled and chopped
1 clove garlic, crushed
150ml/5 fl oz water
2 slices lemon
275ml/10 fl oz mayonnaise
Salt and pepper

Heat the oil, and fry the garlic and onion gently until soft but not coloured. Add the saffron powder and paprika, and cook for 2 minutes. Stir in the tomato purée and water. Add the lemon slices, and salt and pepper to taste. Cook slowly for 10 minutes and then bring to the boil; simmer for 2 minutes. Strain and leave to cool. Add the mayonnaise. Meanwhile, cook the pasta in plenty of boiling salted water for 10 minutes, or until tender but still firm. Rinse under cold water and drain well. Toss in lemon juice, and put in a serving dish. Arrange the prawns on top and pour over sauce. Toss well. Sprinkle with paprika.

Courgette Salad

| PREPARATION TIME: 15 minutes |
| COOKING TIME: 15 minutes |
| SERVES: 4 people |

225g/8oz elbow macaroni
4 courgettes, sliced thinly
2 tomatoes, chopped
8 stuffed green olives, sliced
90ml/6 tbsps French dressing

Cook the pasta in lots of boiling salted water for 10 minutes, or until tender but still firm. Rinse in cold water, and drain well. Mix with 3 tbsps French dressing. Leave to cool. Meanwhile, cook the courgettes gently in boiling, lightly-salted water until just tender but still crisp. Drain and rinse under cold water. Leave to cool. Mix together the pasta, courgettes, tomatoes, stuffed olives and 3 tbsps French dressing. Serve chilled.

Red Mullet Salad

| PREPARATION TIME: 15 minutes |
| COOKING TIME: 15 minutes |
| SERVES: 4 people |

4 small, whole red mullet
2 tbsps olive oil
Lemon juice
Small tin anchovy fillets
90g/3oz pitted black olives
2 hard-boiled eggs
1 green pepper
1 chopped shallot
1 clove garlic, crushed
120g/4oz mushrooms
460g/1lb ripe tomatoes
Salt
Pepper
Seasoned flour

DRESSING
2 tbsps red wine vinegar
6 tbsps olive oil
Handful of chopped mixed herbs
   (e.g. basil, oregano, thyme)

Scale and clean the fish, trimming fins but leaving head and tail on. Cut the tomatoes into quarters and remove the cores. Cut eggs into quarters. Cut the olives in half, lengthways. If the mushrooms are small, leave whole; if not, quarter them. Cut the green pepper into thin slices, and cut the anchovies in half, lengthways. Prepare the dressing and add the chopped herbs, garlic and shallot. Put in the mushrooms and leave to marinate in the refrigerator for about 1 hour. Meanwhile, toss the fish in seasoned flour to coat lightly. Heat 2 tbsps olive oil in a frying pan and fry the fish on both sides until cooked through – about 2-3 minutes per side. When cooking the second side, sprinkle over some lemon juice. Season lightly and leave to cool. When ready to serve, add tomatoes, green peppers, eggs and olives to the mushrooms in their marinade, and toss. Pile the salad into a serving dish and arrange the cold, cooked red mullet on top. Garnish with anchovy fillet strips.

Facing page: Prawn and Pasta Salad (top) and Courgette Salad (bottom).

Prawns in Melons

PREPARATION TIME: 25 minutes

SERVES: 4 people

2 small melons
225g/8oz peeled prawns
Juice of ¹/₂ lemon
1 small cucumber
4 medium, skinned tomatoes
45g/1¹/₂ oz toasted flaked almonds
1 orange
60ml/4 tbsps light vegetable oil
Salt and pepper
2 tbsps chopped basil

Pinch of sugar
1 tsp chopped lemon thyme

Cut the melons in half through the middle and remove the seeds. Scoop out the flesh with a melon-baller or spoon, leaving a 5mm/¹/₄-inch border of fruit on the inside of each shell. Cut a thin slice off the bottom of each shell so that they stand upright. Peel the cucumber, cut in half lengthways, then into 1.25cm/¹/₂-inch cubes. Deseed the tomatoes and cut into strips. Peel and segment the orange. Mix the lemon juice and oil

together for the dressing. Add the chopped basil and thyme, a pinch of sugar, and salt and pepper to taste. Toss the fruit and vegetables together with the prawns. Pile ingredients evenly into each melon shell. Chill well and garnish with the almonds.

This page: **Prawns in Melons (top) and Red Mullet Salad (bottom). Facing page: Winter Salami Risotto (top) Prawn and Tomato Salad (centre) and Italian Pâté (bottom).**

Winter Salami Risotto

PREPARATION TIME: 10 minutes

COOKING TIME: 12 minutes

SERVES: 4 people

225g/8oz salami, thinly sliced
120-175g/4-6oz assorted cured Italian
  meats
2 green peppers
1 red pepper
4 large ripe tomatoes
90g/3oz green beans, cooked
8 stuffed olives
150g/5oz medium or long grain rice,
  cooked
45-60ml/3-4 tbsps Italian dressing

Chop some of the meats and roll the remainder. Chop most of the vegetables, leaving a few large pieces for garnish. Slice the stuffed olives. Blend the rice with the dressing, chopped meat, chopped vegetables and olives and put in the bottom of a shallow dish. Top with the larger pieces of vegetables and rolls of meat. Serve with a green salad.

Chicory, Chicken and Mushroom Salad

PREPARATION TIME:
40 minutes, plus standing time

COOKING TIME: 18-20 minutes

SERVES: 4 people

4 chicken breasts, skinned and boned
6 tbsps olive oil
1 clove garlic, peeled and crushed
Salt and freshly ground black pepper
  to taste
2 medium size heads of chicory
4 large cooked asparagus tips
120g/4oz firm white mushrooms,
  thinly sliced
2 tbsps white wine vinegar
1 tbsp chopped fresh sage (optional)

GARNISH
Sprig fresh basil

Slice the chicken breasts thinly. Heat half the olive oil in a large, shallow pan. Add the chicken slices, garlic and salt and pepper to taste and fry gently for 5 minutes; flip the chicken slices over and fry for a further 3-4

minutes. Meanwhile, prepare the salad ingredients. Cut the heads of the chicory into pieces and arrange on a large, flat plate. Arrange the asparagus tips and mushroom slices between the wedges of chicory. Mix the wine vinegar with the remaining olive oil, salt and pepper to taste and the chopped sage. Spoon the dressing evenly over the salad and top with the fried chicken slices and their juices. Garnish with basil. Serve immediately.

Prawn and Tomato Salad

PREPARATION TIME: 15 minutes

SERVES: 4 people

6 tbsps thick mayonnaise
1 tbsp tomato purée
2 tbsps lemon juice
1 tsp grated lemon zest
1 tsp grated onion
2 tsps chopped fresh parsley
Salt and pepper
225g/8oz prawns

GARNISH
4 tomatoes, quartered
1 head lettuce

Mix the mayonnaise, tomato purée, lemon juice, lemon zest, onion, parsley and seasoning together thoroughly. Leave for 2 hours before using. Check the flavour before mixing the prawns with the sauce. Serve garnished with tomato quarters and surrounded with lettuce leaves.

Italian Pâté

PREPARATION TIME: 15 minutes,
plus 1-2 hours refrigeration

COOKING TIME: 2 hours

OVEN TEMPERATURE:
150°C/300°F/Gas Mark 2

SERVES: 6-8 people

225g/8oz chicken livers, minced
460g/1lb pork liver, minced
225g/8oz minced beef
570g/1¼lbs pork, minced
340g/12oz bacon fat, minced
1 tbsp salt
Pepper
1 tsp ground mace

1 tbsp chopped, fresh mixed herbs
2 tbsps sherry
2 tbsps brandy
3 garlic cloves, peeled and crushed
90g/3oz stuffed green olives

Mix together all the ingredients, except the olives, until well blended. Divide the pâté mixture between two well-greased terrines or loaf tins, adding the olives throughout the pâté at different levels. Cover with foil and put in a roasting tin containing 5cm/2 inches of water. Cook for 2 hours in the oven. Leave to cool. Place the pâté in the refrigerator for 1-2 hours, then turn into a serving dish. Serve with a mixed salad.

Turkey Salad

PREPARATION TIME: 20 minutes

COOKING TIME: 4-5 minutes

SERVES: 4-6 people

1 Cos lettuce
Few young spinach leaves
Juice of 1 lemon
90ml/6 tbsps olive oil
2 cloves garlic, crushed
3 drops Tabasco
4 anchovy fillets, chopped
Salt and freshly ground black pepper to
  taste

Chicory, Chicken and Mushroom Salad (above right) and Turkey Salad (right).

1 egg
2 slices bread, cut into small cubes
175g/6oz cooked turkey, cut into thin strips

Tear the lettuce into pieces and put into a salad bowl with the young spinach leaves. Mix the lemon juice with 3 tbsps of the olive oil, half the garlic, Tabasco, anchovies and salt and pepper to taste. Put the egg into a pan of boiling water and cook for just 45 seconds – the white and yolk must still be very runny. Carefully crack the egg into the dressing, beating well. Heat the remaining olive oil with the rest of the garlic in a frying pan; add the bread cubes and fry until crisp and golden. Add the croûtons, turkey strips and prepared dressing to the salad greens and toss well together. Serve immediately.

Gianfottere Salad

PREPARATION TIME: 40 minutes

COOKING TIME: 30 minutes

SERVES: 4 people

225g/8oz pasta spirals
1 aubergine
1 courgette
1 red pepper
1 green pepper
2 tomatoes
1 onion
60ml/4 tbsps olive oil
1 clove garlic
Salt
Pepper

Cut the aubergine into 1cm/¹/₂ inch-slices. Sprinkle with salt and leave for 30 minutes. Skin the tomatoes by putting them into boiling water for 20 seconds and then rinsing in cold water and peeling skins off. Chop roughly. Cut the courgette into 1cm/¹/₂-inch slices. Remove the cores and seeds from the peppers, and chop roughly. Peel and chop the onion. Heat 45ml/3 tbsps olive oil in a pan, and fry the onion gently until transparent, but not coloured. Meanwhile, rinse salt from the aubergine and pat dry with kitchen

paper. Chop roughly. Add the aubergine, courgette, peppers, tomatoes and garlic to the onion, and fry gently for 20 minutes. Season with salt and pepper. Allow to cool. Meanwhile, cook the pasta spirals in plenty of boiling salted water for 10 minutes, or until tender but still firm. Rinse in cold water and drain well; toss in the remaining 15ml/1 tbsp olive oil. Toss the vegetables together with the pasta spirals.

Mushroom Salad

PREPARATION TIME:
1 hour 10 minutes

COOKING TIME: 15 minutes

SERVES: 4 people

225g/8oz farfalle (pasta bows)
225g/8oz button mushrooms, sliced
75ml/5 tbsps olive oil

Juice of 2 lemons
1 tsp fresh chopped basil
1 tsp fresh chopped parsley
Salt
Pepper

Mix the oil together with the lemon juice and fresh herbs. Put the sliced mushrooms into a bowl and pour over 60ml/4 tbsps of the dressing. Leave for 1 hour. Cook the pasta in a large saucepan of boiling salted water for 10 minutes, or until tender. Rinse in cold water, and drain. Toss with the rest of the dressing, and leave to cool. Fold the mushrooms and pasta together gently, adding salt and freshly ground black pepper to taste. Sprinkle with parsley.

This page: Gianfottere Salad. Facing page: Fisherman's Wholemeal Pasta Salad.

Prawn Salad

PREPARATION TIME: 10 minutes

COOKING TIME: 15 minutes

SERVES: 4 people

225g/8oz pasta shells
225g/8oz prawns, shelled and deveined
150ml/¹/₄ pint mayonnaise
Juice of 1 lemon
1 tsp paprika
Salt
Pepper
1 lettuce
1 cucumber, sliced

Cook the pasta in plenty of boiling salted water for 10 minutes, or until tender. Drain, and rinse under cold water. Shake off the excess water; put into a bowl, and pour over the lemon juice. Leave to cool. Mix the paprika into the mayonnaise. Add to the prawns, and toss. Arrange a bed of lettuce leaves and sliced cucumber in a dish and pile the pasta in the centre. Pile the prawns on top. (This can also be made with flaked crabmeat or salmon).

Fisherman's Wholemeal Pasta Salad

PREPARATION TIME:
20 minutes, plus cooling time

COOKING TIME: about 10 minutes

SERVES: 4 people

225g/8oz wholemeal pasta shapes
  (shells, wheels, etc)
Salt and freshly ground black pepper to
  taste
4 tbsps olive oil
2 tbsps dry white wine
1 tbsp chopped parsley
3 spring onions, chopped
120g/4oz shelled, cooked mussels
90g/3oz peeled prawns
120g/4oz flaked crabmeat
12 black olives

GARNISH
King prawns

Cook the wholewheat pasta in a large pan of boiling salted water until just tender – about 10 minutes. Meanwhile, prepare the dressing. Mix the olive oil with the white wine, parsley, and salt and pepper to taste. Drain the cooked pasta thoroughly and stir in the prepared dressing. Allow to cool. Mix in the chopped spring onion and then carefully stir in the seafood; add the black olives. Spoon into one large salad bowl or four individual ones.

Prawn Salad (left) and Mushroom
Salad (far left)

Bean Salad

PREPARATION TIME: 10 minutes

COOKING TIME: 15 minutes

SERVES: 4 people

225g/8oz penne
425g/15oz tin red kidney beans, drained
60g/2oz bacon, rind removed, sliced
1 onion, peeled and chopped
2 sticks celery, sliced diagonally
1-2 tbsps wine vinegar
3-4 tbsps olive oil
1 tsp chopped parsley
Salt
Pepper

Cook the penne in plenty of salted boiling water for 10 minutes, or until 'al dente'. Rinse in cold water and drain well. Heat a frying pan and sauté the bacon in its own fat until crisp. Add the onion, with a little oil if necessary, and cook until soft. Mix together the vinegar, oil, and parsley, and season well. Add the bacon, onion, kidney beans and celery to the penne. Pour the dressing over and toss together.

Chickpea, Mint and Orange Salad

PREPARATION TIME: 15-25 minutes

SERVES: 4 people

175g/6oz dried chickpeas, soaked
overnight and cooked
2 tbsps chopped fresh mint
1 clove garlic, crushed
Salt and pepper to taste

Juice of 1 orange
Rind of 1 orange, cut into matchstick
strips
3 tbsps olive oil
2 large oranges, rind and pith removed,
flesh segmented

GARNISH
Fresh mint leaves

Mix the chickpeas with half the chopped mint, garlic, and salt and pepper to taste. Mix the orange juice, strips of rind and olive oil together; stir into the chickpeas. Lightly mix in the orange segments and garnish with the remaining chopped mint.

Tuna and Tomato Salad

PREPARATION TIME: 10 minutes

COOKING TIME: 15 minutes

SERVES: 4 people

225g/8oz pasta shells
200g/7oz tin tuna fish, flaked
6 tomatoes
1 tbsp fresh chopped basil or marjoram,
or 1 tsp dried basil or oregano
90ml/6 tbsps French dressing

Mix the herbs with the French dressing. Cook the pasta shells in a large saucepan of boiling salted water until tender – about 10 minutes. Rinse with cold water and drain, shaking off the excess water. Toss with 45ml/3 tbsps of French dressing. Leave to cool. Meanwhile, slice enough of the tomatoes to arrange around the outside of the serving dish. Chop the rest, and pour the remaining French dressing over them, and place in the centre of the dish. Add the tuna to the pasta shells and toss gently. Serve in the centre of the dish over the chopped tomatoes.

This page: **Chickpea, Mint and Orange Salad (top)** and **Spinach and Fontina Cheese Lasagne (bottom).** Facing page: **Bean Salad (top)** and **Tuna and Tomato Salad (bottom).**

Spinach and Fontina Cheese Lasagne

PREPARATION TIME: 20-25 minutes

COOKING TIME: about 35 minutes

OVEN TEMPERATURE:
190°C/375°F/Gas Mark 5

SERVES: 6 people

460g/1lb cooked and drained spinach
    (or thawed frozen spinach)
Generous pinch grated nutmeg
Salt and freshly ground black pepper to
    taste
2 tbsps cream
1 clove garlic, crushed
1 egg yolks
175g/6oz fontina cheese, grated
225g/8oz green or wholewheat lasagne
    (the non pre-cook variety)

SAUCE
140ml/¼ pint double cream
1 egg, beaten
2 tbsps grated Parmesan cheese
3 firm tomatoes, sliced

Mix the cooked spinach with nutmeg and salt and pepper to taste; stir in the cream, garlic, egg yolk and grated fontina. Layer the lasagne and spinach mixture in a lightly greased ovenproof dish, starting with spinach and finishing with lasagne. For the sauce: mix the cream with the beaten egg and half the grated Parmesan; spoon over the lasagne. Top with the sliced tomato and the remaining Parmesan. Bake in the oven for about 35 minutes, or until golden. Serve piping hot.

Chicken Salad with Pasta Shells

PREPARATION TIME: 10 minutes

COOKING TIME: 15 minutes

SERVES: 4 people

120g/4oz pasta shells
225g/8oz cooked chicken, shredded
1 x 200g/7oz tin corn, drained
1 stick celery, sliced
1 sweet red pepper, cored, seeds
    removed, and diced
1 green pepper, cored, seeds removed,
    and diced

DRESSING
1 tbsp mayonnaise
2 tbsps vinegar
Salt
Pepper

Cook the pasta in plenty of boiling salted water until just tender. Drain well and leave to cool. Meanwhile, combine the mayonnaise with the vinegar and salt and pepper to taste. When the pasta is cool, add the chicken, corn, celery and peppers. Toss well and serve with the dressing.

Rice and Tuna Stuffed Aubergines

PREPARATION TIME: 40 minutes

COOKING TIME: about 50 minutes

OVEN TEMPERATURE:
190°C/375°F/Gas Mark 5

SERVES: 4 people

4 small aubergines
3 tbsps olive oil
Salt and freshly ground black pepper
    to taste
1 small onion, finely chopped
1 clove garlic, peeled and crushed
6 tbsps cooked brown rice
1 x 200g/7oz tin tuna, drained and
    coarsely flaked

This page: Chicken Salad with Pasta Shells. Facing page: Courgette, Caper and Anchovy Salad (top) and Rice and Tuna Stuffed Aubergines (bottom).

1 tbsp mayonnaise
4 tomatoes, skinned, seeded and chopped
1 tbsp coarsely chopped parsley

Cut the aubergines in half lengthways. Score the cut surfaces lightly with a sharp knife at regular intervals. Brush lightly with oil and sprinkle with salt. Place on a greased baking sheet and bake in the oven for 15 minutes. Carefully scoop the centre flesh from each half of the aubergine, making sure that you do not break the skin. Fry the chopped onion gently in 2 tbsps of the olive oil for 3 minutes. Add the garlic, scooped aubergine flesh, and salt and pepper to taste; fry gently for a further 2 minutes. Add the rice, flaked tuna, mayonnaise, chopped tomato and parsley, and mix together. Fill the aubergine 'shells' with the rice mixture and place in a lightly greased ovenproof dish. Sprinkle with the remaining olive oil. Bake in the oven for about 25 minutes. Serve piping hot.

Courgette, Caper and Anchovy Salad

PREPARATION TIME: 15-20 minutes
SERVES: 4 people

460g/1lb courgettes
1 small onion, thinly sliced
1 tbsp capers
4-6 anchovies, chopped
1 tbsp anchovy oil (drained from the tin of anchovies)
2 tbsps olive oil
2 tbsps tarragon vinegar
Juice of 1/2 lemon
Salt and freshly ground black pepper to taste

GARNISH
3 sprigs rosemary
2 whole anchovies

The secret of this salad is to slice the raw courgettes really thinly – you can do this with a sharp knife, but it is much easier if you use the slicing blade on a food processor or a mandolin. Trim the courgettes and slice very thinly. Mix with the onion, capers and chopped anchovies. Mix the anchovy oil, olive oil, tarragon vinegar and lemon juice together; add salt and pepper to taste. Stir the dressing into the prepared salad ingredients and garnish with anchovies and rosemary.

Stuffed Tomatoes

PREPARATION TIME: 10 minutes
COOKING TIME: 20 minutes
OVEN TEMPERATURE: 180°C/350°F/Gas Mark 4
SERVES: 4 people

4 large ripe tomatoes
460g/1lb fresh spinach
60g/2oz soup pasta
30g/1oz butter, softened
1 tbsp double cream
1/4 tsp grated nutmeg
1 clove garlic, crushed
Salt and pepper
1 tbsp Parmesan or Cheddar cheese, grated
4 anchovy fillets, halved lengthways

Cut the tops off the tomatoes and carefully scoop out the insides with a teaspoon. Wash the spinach well and remove the stalks. Cook gently in a large saucepan, without added water, until the spinach is soft. Chop the spinach very finely or blend in a food processor. Squeeze to remove excess moisture. Meanwhile, cook the pasta in boiling water for 5 minutes, or until 'al dente'. Rinse and drain well. Mix with the spinach. Add the butter, cream, nutmeg and garlic, and season well. Fill each tomato and top with the cheese and anchovies. Bake in an oven for 10 minutes. Serve immediately.

Stuffed Courgettes

PREPARATION TIME: 15 minutes
COOKING TIME: 30 minutes
OVEN TEMPERATURE: 200°C/400°F/Gas Mark 6
SERVES: 4 people

4 courgettes
60g/2oz soup pasta
2 tomatoes, skin removed, chopped and seeds removed
2 tbsps butter or margarine
120g/4oz minced beef
1 small onion, peeled and chopped
2 cloves garlic, crushed
60g/2oz fontina cheese, grated
1 tbsp breadcrumbs
1 tsp tomato purée
Salt and pepper

Cook the pasta in lots of boiling salted water for 5 minutes or until tender. Rinse in cold water and drain well. Meanwhile, put the courgettes in a pan and cover with cold water. Bring to the boil and cook gently for 3 minutes. Rinse under cold water. Cut the courgettes in half, lengthways. Carefully scoop out the pulp, leaving 1.25cm/1/2-inch thickness on skin. Chop the pulp. Heat the butter in a frying pan. Add the garlic and onion and fry gently until transparent. Increase the heat and add the minced beef. Fry for 5 minutes, stirring often until meat is well browned. Stir in the tomato purée and salt and pepper to taste. Add the courgette pulp, tomatoes and pasta, and cook for 2 minutes. Spoon into the courgette shells. Sprinkle the top with grated cheese and breadcrumbs, and brown under a grill or in a hot oven. Serve immediately.

Mushrooms and Tomatoes

PREPARATION TIME: 10 minutes, plus chilling time
COOKING TIME: about 13 minutes
SERVES: 4 people

460g/1lb tomatoes, skinned, seeded and chopped
140ml/5 fl oz red wine
2 tbsps tomato purée
Salt and freshly ground black pepper to taste
1 clove garlic, peeled and finely chopped
2 spring onions, finely chopped
2 tbsps sultanas

Facing page: Stuffed Tomatoes (top) and Stuffed Courgette (bottom).

225g/8oz button mushrooms

TO SERVE
Crusty bread or rolls

Put the chopped tomatoes, red wine, tomato purée, salt and pepper to taste and the garlic into a shallow pan. Simmer for 6-8 minutes. Add the spring onions, sultanas and mushrooms; cover the pan and simmer for 5 minutes. Allow to cool and then chill very thoroughly. Serve in small, shallow dishes, accompanied by crusty bread.

Fennel au Gratin

PREPARATION TIME: 15 minutes
COOKING TIME: 25-30 minute
OVEN TEMPERATURE:
190°C/375°F/Gas Mark 5
SERVES: 4 people

4 medium bulbs of fennel
Juice of 1 lemon
Salt and freshly ground black pepper
to taste
30g/1oz butter
25g/³/4 oz flour
140ml/¹/4 pint milk
140ml/¹/4 pint dry white wine
60ml/4 tbsps cream
90g/3oz grated fontina cheese

GARNISH
1 tbsp chopped chives

Trim both ends of the fennel – reserve any feathery fronds for garnish. Peel off any discoloured patches from the fennel. Cut each in half lengthways. Put the fennel into a pan of boiling water to which you have added the lemon juice and 1 tsp salt; simmer steadily for 5 minutes. Drain the part-boiled fennel thoroughly. Melt the butter in a pan and stir in the flour; gradually stir in the milk and white wine. Bring to the boil and stir until slightly thickened. Beat in the cream, half the grated cheese and salt and pepper to taste. Arrange the fennel in a lightly greased ovenproof dish and spoon the sauce evenly over the top; sprinkle with the remaining cheese.

Bake in a preheated oven for 25-30 minutes, or until the sauce is golden. Garnish with the chopped chives and any reserved fronds from the fennel.

Stuffed Aubergines

PREPARATION TIME: 15 minutes
COOKING TIME: 1 hour
SERVES: 4 people

4 small or 2 large aubergines
60g/2oz macaroni
225g/8oz bacon, diced
1 green pepper, cored and diced
1 yellow pepper, cored and diced
2 tomatoes, skin removed, chopped
and seeds removed
2 tbsps butter
¹/2 tsp chilli powder
1 tbsp tomato purée
1 small onion, peeled and chopped
1 clove garlic, crushed
60g/2oz Mozzarella cheese, grated
1 tbsp breadcrumbs
Salt and pepper

Cook the macaroni in plenty of boiling salted water for 10 minutes, or until tender but still firm. Rinse in cold water, and drain well. Wrap the aubergines in baking foil and bake in an oven preheated to 180°C/375°F/ Gas Mark 5 for 30 minutes. Cut the aubergines in half, lengthways. Scoop out the pulp, leaving 1.25cm/¹/2-inch thickness on the skin. Chop the pulp. Heat the butter in a pan. Add the onion and garlic and cook until transparent. Add the bacon and peppers and fry for 5 minutes. Then add the aubergine pulp, tomatoes, tomato purée, chilli powder, and salt and pepper. Cook for a further 3 minutes. Stir in the macaroni, and fill the scooped-out aubergine halves with the mixture. Top with grated cheese and breadcrumbs and brown under a grill or in a quick oven at 200°C/400°F/Gas Mark 6. Serve immediately.

This page: Mushrooms and Tomatoes (top) and Fennel au Gratin (bottom). Facing page: Stuffed Aubergines.

ITALIAN COOKING

PASTA DISHES

Spaghetti with Basil Sauce (Pesto)

PREPARATION TIME: 5 minutes

COOKING TIME: 15 minutes

SERVES: 4 people

75ml/5 tbsps olive oil
2 cloves garlic, crushed
2 tbsps pine nuts
120g/4oz fresh basil leaves
3 tbsps Parmesan or pecorino cheese, grated
Salt and pepper
275g/10oz spaghetti

GARNISH
Fresh basil

Heat 1 tbsp of the oil over a low heat, add the garlic and pine nuts and cook until the pine nuts are a light golden brown. Drain. Finely chop the basil leaves, pine nuts and garlic in a food processor with a metal blade, or in a blender. When smooth, add the remaining oil in a thin stream, blending continuously. Turn mixture into a bowl and stir in the cheese, adding the salt and pepper to taste. Meanwhile, cook the spaghetti in a large pan of boiling salted water for 10 minutes, or until 'al dente'. Drain, and serve with the pesto tossed through. Serve with a side dish of grated cheese. Garnish with fresh basil.

This page: Tagliatelle with Garlic and Oil (top) and Spaghetti with Basil Sauce (Pesto) (bottom). Facing page: Spinach Ravioli (top) and Meat Ravioli (bottom).

Tagliatelle with Garlic and Oil

PREPARATION TIME: 5 minutes

COOKING TIME: 10 minutes

SERVES: 4 people

275g/10oz green tagliatelle
140ml/¼ pint olive oil
3 cloves garlic, crushed
2 tbsps chopped parsley
Salt and pepper

Cook the tagliatelle in lots of boiling salted water for 10 minutes, or until tender but still firm, stirring occasionally. Meanwhile, make the sauce. Heat the oil in a pan and, when warm, add the garlic. Fry gently until softened. Add the chopped parsley, and salt and pepper to taste. Drain the tagliatelle. Add the sauce and toss to coat well. Serve hot.

Spinach Ravioli

PREPARATION TIME: 30 minutes

COOKING TIME: 20 minutes

SERVES: 4 people

DOUGH
250g/9oz strong plain flour
Pinch of salt
3 eggs

FILLING
225g/8oz cooked spinach
30g/1oz butter or margarine
60g/2oz Parmesan cheese, grated
Pinch of grated nutmeg
1 egg, beaten
Salt
Pepper

CREAM CHEESE SAUCE
30g/1oz butter or margarine
15g/½oz flour
300ml/½ pint milk
1 tsp French mustard
2 tbsps grated Parmesan cheese

TO MAKE THE FILLING
Chop the spinach and heat in a pan. Beat the butter into the spinach. Add the Parmesan cheese, nutmeg and salt and freshly-ground black pepper to taste. Finally mix in the beaten egg.

TO MAKE THE DOUGH
Sift the flour in a bowl; make a well in the centre and add the eggs. Work the flour and the eggs together with a spoon, and then knead by hand until a smooth dough is formed. Leave to rest for 15 minutes. Lightly flour a board and roll out dough thinly into a rectangle. Cut the dough in half. Shape the filling into small balls and set them about 4cm/1½-inches apart on one half of the dough. Place the other half on top, and cut with a ravioli cutter or small pastry cutter. Seal the edges. Cook in batches in a large, wide pan with plenty of boiling salted water until tender – about 8 minutes. Remove carefully with a slotted spoon. Meanwhile, make the sauce.

TO MAKE THE SAUCE
Heat the butter in a pan. Sift in the flour and cook for 30 seconds. Draw off the heat, and stir in the milk gradually. Bring to the boil and simmer for 3 minutes, stirring continuously. Add the mustard and half the cheese, and seasoning to taste.

Pour the sauce over the ravioli and serve immediately with the remaining cheese sprinkled over the top.

Meat Ravioli

PREPARATION TIME: 30 minutes

COOKING TIME: 30 minutes

SERVES: 4 people

DOUGH
250g/9oz strong plain flour
Pinch of salt
3 eggs

FILLING
60g/2oz butter or margarine
1 clove garlic, crushed
1 onion, peeled and grated
225g/8oz minced beef
75ml/5 tbsps red wine
2 tbsps breadcrumbs
120g/4oz cooked spinach, chopped
2 eggs, beaten
Salt and pepper

SAUCE
1 x 400g/14oz tin plum tomatoes
1 small onion, peeled and grated
1 small carrot, diced finely
1 bay leaf
3 parsley stalks
Salt and pepper

60g/2oz Parmesan cheese, grated

TO MAKE THE FILLING
Heat the butter in a pan. Add the garlic and the onion and fry gently for 1 minute. Add the minced beef and fry until browned. Add the red wine and salt and pepper to taste, and cook uncovered for 15 minutes. Strain the juices and reserve them for the sauce. Allow to cool. Add the breadcrumbs, chopped spinach, and beaten eggs to bind.

TO MAKE THE DOUGH
Sift the flour in a bowl. Make a well in the centre and add the eggs. Work the flour and eggs together with a spoon, then knead by hand until a smooth dough is formed. Leave dough to rest for 15 minutes. Lightly flour a board, and roll the dough thinly into a rectangle. Cut the dough in half. Shape the filling into small balls, and set them about 4cm/1½-inches apart on one half of the dough. Place the other half on top, and cut with a ravioli cutter or small pastry cutter. Seal the edges. Cook in batches in a large, wide pan in plenty of boiling salted water until tender – about 8 minutes. Remove carefully with a slotted spoon. Meanwhile, make the sauce.

TO MAKE THE SAUCE
Put all the ingredients in a saucepan. Add the juice from the cooked meat, and bring to the boil. Simmer for 10 minutes. Push through a sieve and return the smooth sauce to the pan. Adjust seasoning.

Put the ravioli in a warm dish and cover with tomato sauce. Serve immediately, with grated Parmesan cheese.

Facing page: Spaghetti Neapolitana (top) and Farfalle with Creamy Cheese Sauce (bottom).

Farfalle with Creamy Cheese Sauce

PREPARATION TIME: 5 minutes

COOKING TIME: 15 minutes

SERVES: 4 people

275g/10oz farfalle (pasta bows)
15g/½oz butter or margarine
15g/½oz flour
300ml/½ pint milk
60g/2oz Gruyère or Cheddar cheese, grated
½ tsp French mustard
1 tbsp grated Parmesan cheese

Heat the butter in a pan. Stir in the flour and cook for 1 minute. Remove from the heat and gradually stir in the milk. Return to the heat and stir continuously. Boil for 3 minutes. Stir in the Gruyère or Cheddar cheese and mustard; do not reboil. Meanwhile, cook the pasta in lots of boiling salted water for 10 minutes, or until tender but still firm. Rinse in hot water and drain well. Pour over the cheese sauce, and toss. Top with a sprinkling of Parmesan cheese. Serve immediately.

Spaghetti Neapolitana

PREPARATION TIME: 5 minutes

COOKING TIME: 30 minutes

SERVES: 4 people

275g/10oz spaghetti
2 x 400g/14oz tins plum tomatoes
30ml/2 tbsps olive oil
12 tsp oregano or marjoram
Salt
Pepper
2 tbsps chopped parsley
Parmesan cheese, grated

Push undrained tomatoes through a sieve. Heat oil in a pan. Add oregano or marjoram, and cook for 30 seconds Add the puréed tomatoes, and salt and pepper. Bring to the boil; reduce the heat; simmer uncovered for 20-30 minutes. Meanwhile, cook the spaghetti in lots of boiling salted water for about 10 minutes, or until tender but still firm. Rinse under hot water, and drain well. Pour the tomato sauce over the spaghetti, and toss gently. Sprinkle the parsley over the top. Serve with Parmesan cheese. Serve immediately.

Wholemeal Spaghetti with Peas and Bacon

PREPARATION TIME: 10 minutes

COOKING TIME: 15 minutes

SERVES: 4 people

275g/10oz wholemeal spaghetti
350g/12oz peas
1 tsp sugar
120g/4oz bacon, rind removed, and diced
90g/3oz butter or margarine
Salt and pepper

GARNISH
Parsley

Cook the spaghetti in lots of boiling salted water for 10 minutes, or until tender but still firm. Drain. Meanwhile, cook the peas in boiling water with a pinch of salt and a teaspoon of sugar. Melt the butter in a pan and fry the bacon. When crisp, add the peas, and salt and pepper to taste, and pour over the spaghetti. Toss through and serve immediately, garnished with chopped parsley if desired.

Penne with Anchovy Sauce

PREPARATION TIME: 15 minutes

COOKING TIME: 20 minutes

SERVES: 4 people

6-8 anchovies, drained
2 tbsps olive oil
1 x 400g/14oz tin tomatoes, chopped
3 tbsps chopped parsley
Pepper
275g/10oz penne
30g/1oz butter or margarine
30g/1oz Parmesan cheese, grated

Chop the anchovies and cook them in the oil, stirring to a paste. Add the chopped tomatoes to the anchovies, with the parsley and freshly-ground black pepper to taste. Bring to the boil and simmer, uncovered, for 10 minutes. Meanwhile, cook the penne in lots of boiling salted water for 10 minutes, or until 'al dente'. Rinse in hot water and drain well. Toss in the butter. Combine the sauce with the pasta, sprinkle with some extra chopped parsley, and serve immediately with the grated Parmesan cheese.

Penne with Anchovy Sauce (left) and Wholemeal Spaghetti with Peas and Bacon (below).

Fish Ravioli

PREPARATION TIME: 30 minutes

COOKING TIME: 30 minutes

OVEN TEMPERATURE:
180°C/350°F/Gas Mark 4

SERVES: 4 people

PASTA DOUGH
275g/10oz strong plain flour
Pinch of salt
3 eggs

FILLING
225g/8oz sole fillets, or flounder,
*   skinned and boned*
1 slice of onion
1 slice of lemon
6 peppercorns
1 bay leaf
1 tbsp lemon juice
225ml/8 fl oz water
2 eggs, beaten
2 tbsps breadcrumbs
1 spring onion, finely chopped
Salt and pepper

LEMON SAUCE
30g/1oz butter or margarine
2 tbsps flour
225ml/8 fl oz strained cooking liquid
from fish
2 tbsps double cream
Salt and pepper
2 tbsps lemon juice

TO MAKE THE FILLING
Place the fish in an ovenproof dish
with the onion, slice of lemon,
peppercorns, bay leaf, lemon juice
and water. Cover and cook in a
preheated oven for 20 minutes.
Remove the fish from liquid and
allow to drain. Strain the liquid and
set aside. When the fish is cool, beat
with the back of a spoon to a pulp.
Add the eggs, breadcrumbs, spring
onion and salt and pepper to taste.
Mix well.

TO MAKE THE DOUGH
Sift the flour into a bowl, add the salt,
then make a well in the centre and
add the eggs. Work the flour and eggs
together with a spoon, and then
knead by hand until a smooth dough

is formed. Leave to rest for 15
minutes. Lightly flour a board and roll
out the dough into a rectangle until it
is thin enough to see through. Cut
the dough in half. Shape the filling
into small balls and set them about
4cm/1½-inches apart on one half of
the dough. Place the other half on
top, and cut with a ravioli cutter or
small pastry cutter. Seal the edges.
Cook in batches in a large, wide pan
in plenty of boiling salted water for
about 8 minutes or until tender.
Remove carefully with a slotted
spoon. Meanwhile, make the sauce.

TO MAKE THE SAUCE
Melt the butter in a pan. Stir in the
flour and cook for 30 seconds. Draw
off the heat and gradually stir in the
liquid from the cooked fish. Return to

the heat and bring to the boil.
Simmer for 4 minutes, stirring
continuously. Add the cream and mix
well. Season to taste. Remove from
the heat and gradually stir in the
lemon juice. Do not reboil. Pour the
sauce over the ravioli and serve
immediately.

Ravioli with Ricotta Cheese

PREPARATION TIME: 30 minutes

COOKING TIME: 20 minutes

SERVES: 4 people

DOUGH
250g/9oz strong plain flour
Pinch of salt
3 eggs

FILLING
30g/1oz butter or margarine
1 egg yolk
225g/8oz ricotta cheese
60g/2oz Parmesan cheese, grated
2 tbsps chopped parsley
Salt and pepper

TOMATO SAUCE
15ml/1 tbsp olive oil
1 small onion, peeled and chopped
30g/1oz bacon
1 bay leaf
1 tsp basil
1 tbsp flour
1 x 400g/14oz tin plum tomatoes
Salt and pepper
15ml/1 tbsp double cream

TO MAKE THE FILLING
Beat the butter to a cream, add the egg yolk and blend well. Beat the ricotta cheese to a cream and add the butter-egg mixture gradually until smooth. Add the Parmesan cheese, parsley and salt and pepper to taste. Set aside.

TO MAKE THE DOUGH
Sift the flour in a bowl. Make a well in the centre, and add the eggs. Work the flour and eggs together with a spoon, and then knead by hand until a smooth dough is formed. Leave to rest for 15 minutes. Lightly flour a board and roll dough out thinly into a rectangle. Cut the dough in half. Shape the filling into small balls and set them about 4cm/ 1½-inches apart on one half of the dough. Place the other half on top and cut with a ravioli cutter or small pastry cuter. Seal the edges. Cook in batches in a large, wide pan in plenty of boiling salted water until tender – about 8 minutes. Remove carefully with a slotted spoon. Meanwhile, make the sauce.

TO MAKE THE SAUCE
Heat the oil and fry the bacon and onion until golden. Add the bay leaf and basil and stir in the flour. Cook for 1 minute, draw off the heat and add tomatoes gradually, stirring continuously. Add salt and pepper to taste. Return to the heat and bring to the boil. Cook for 5 minutes, then push through a sieve. Stir in the cream and adjust the seasoning. Pour the sauce over the ravioli. Serve immediately.

Facing page: Fish Ravioli. This page: Ravioli with Ricotta Cheese (left), Brasciole with Tagliatelle (centre) and Hare Sauce with Wholemeal Spaghetti (right).

Hare Sauce with Wholemeal Spaghetti

PREPARATION TIME: 10 minutes

COOKING TIME: 1 hour 15 minutes

SERVES: 4 people

30ml/2 tbsps olive oil
225g/8oz hare, cut into small pieces
2 onions, peeled and sliced
120g/4oz streaky bacon rashers, rind removed, and diced
1 clove garlic, crushed
1/2 tsp oregano
15g/1/2oz flour
150ml/1/4 pint red wine
275g/10oz wholemeal spaghetti
Salt and pepper

Heat the oil in a heavy pan. Lightly brown the hare pieces. Remove and put aside. Add the onion, bacon, garlic and oregano to the oil and fry until lightly coloured. Draw off the heat and stir in the flour with a metal spoon. Return to the heat and cook for 2 minutes. Remove from the heat and add the wine and return to the heat, stirring until boiling. Add the hare, cover the pan and simmer gently for about 1 hour, until the hare is tender. Add the salt and pepper to taste. When the sauce is ready, cook the spaghetti in lots of boiling salted water for about 10 minutes, or until tender but still firm. Rinse in hot water and drain. Serve with the hare sauce on top. Serve immediately.

Brasciole with Tagliatelle

PREPARATION TIME: 15 minutes

COOKING TIME: 25 minutes

SERVES: 4 people

4 veal steaks
4 thin slices ham
30g/4 tbsps grated Parmesan cheese
Salt and pepper
30g/1oz butter or margarine
1 x 400g/14oz tin tomatoes, sieved
225g/8oz tagliatelle

Bat the veal steaks thinly between two sheets of dampened greaseproof paper. Place a slice of ham on the top of each steak and sprinkle each with a tablespoon of the Parmesan cheese and some freshly ground black pepper.

Roll up from a short side, like a Swiss roll, tucking the slices in to form neat parcels. Tie gently with string at each end and in the middle. Heat the butter in a pan and add the veal rolls. Cook gently until lightly browned all over. Add the sieved tomatoes, cover and cook for 15 minutes. Meanwhile, cook the tagliatelle in plenty of boiling salted water for 10 minutes, or until tender but still firm. Rinse in hot water and drain. Cut the veal rolls into 2.5cm/1-inch rounds. Toss the tagliatelle together with the tomato sauce and top with the veal rolls and the grated Parmesan cheese. Serve immediately.

Wholemeal Spaghetti with Walnuts and Parsley

PREPARATION TIME: 10 minutes

COOKING TIME: 10 minutes

SERVES: 4 people

2 cloves garlic, peeled
60ml/4 tbsps olive oil
4 tbsps fresh parsley
2 tbsps walnuts
3 tbsps grated Parmesan or pecorino cheese
Salt and pepper
275g/10oz wholewheat spaghetti

Fry the garlic gently in oil for 2 minutes. Set the oil aside to cool. Wash the parsley and remove the stalks. Finely chop the parsley, walnuts and garlic in a food processor with a metal blade, or in a blender. When chopped well, add the cooled oil in a thin stream. Turn the mixture into a bowl, mix in the grated cheese and add the salt and pepper to taste. Cook the spaghetti in a large pan of boiling salted water for 10 minutes or until tender but still firm. Drain. Serve with the sauce tossed through. Serve with a side dish of grated Parmesan or pecorino cheese.

Tagliatelle with Bacon and Tomato Sauce

PREPARATION TIME: 15 minutes

COOKING TIME: 15 minutes

SERVES: 4 people

15ml/1 tbsp olive oil

1 onion, peeled and finely chopped
6 rashers of bacon, rind removed, and cut into strips
2 tbsps chopped parsley
1 tbsp dry basil
1 x 400g/14oz tin plum tomatoes, drained, seeds removed, and chopped roughly
Salt and pepper
275g/10oz red tagliatelle
60g/2oz pecorino cheese, grated

Heat the oil in a pan. Add the onion and bacon and cook over a gentle heat until the onion is transparent but not coloured. Add the parsley, basil and tomato. Simmer gently for 5 minutes, stirring occasionally. Add salt and pepper to taste. Meanwhile, cook the tagliatelle in a large pan with plenty of boiling salted water. Cook for about 10 minutes, until tender but still firm. Drain and return to the pan. Add the sauce and toss through. Serve with grated pecorino cheese.

Tagliatelle with Bacon and Tomato
Sauce (left) and Wholemeal Spaghetti
with Walnuts and Parsley (below).

Pasta Spirals with Peas and Tomatoes

PREPARATION TIME: 5 minutes

COOKING TIME: 15 minutes

SERVES: 4 people

275g/10oz pasta spirals
350g/12oz peas
1 tsp sugar
60g/2oz butter or margarine
1 tsp basil
1 x 400g/14oz tin plum tomatoes, chopped
Salt and pepper

Cook the pasta spirals in plenty of boiling salted water for 10 minutes or until tender. Drain. Meanwhile, cook the peas in boiling water with a pinch of salt and a teaspoon of sugar. Melt the butter in a pan. Add the basil and cook for 30 seconds. Add the tomatoes and their juice. When hot, add the pasta spirals, peas and salt and pepper to taste. Toss together. Serve immediately.

Farfalle with Tomato Sauce

PREPARATION TIME: 10 minutes

COOKING TIME: 30 minutes

SERVES: 4 people

15ml/1 tbsp olive oil
2 cloves garlic, crushed
1 onion, peeled and sliced
1/2 tsp dry basil
1 x 400g/14oz tin plum tomatoes, chopped
Salt and pepper
275g/10oz farfalle
2 tbsps chopped fresh basil or chopped parsley

Parmesan cheese, grated

Heat the oil in a pan. Add the garlic and onion, and cook until softened. Add the dry basil and cook for 30 seconds. Add the undrained tomatoes; season with salt and pepper. Bring to the boil, reduce the heat and simmer, uncovered, for about 20 minutes, or until the sauce is reduced by half. Meanwhile, cook the pasta in a large pan of boiling salted water until tender but still firm – about 10 minutes. Rinse in hot water and drain well. Put the sauce through a sieve and stir in the fresh parsley or basil. Toss the sauce through the pasta. Serve with grated Parmesan cheese. Serve immediately.

Pasta Shells with Mushroom Sauce

PREPARATION TIME: 5 minutes

COOKING TIME: 15 minutes

SERVES: 4 people

30g/1oz butter
225g/8oz button mushrooms
15g/1/2oz flour
600ml/1 pint milk
Salt and pepper
275g/10oz pasta shells

Rinse the mushrooms and chop them roughly. Melt the butter in a saucepan and add mushrooms. Fry for 5 minutes, stirring occasionally. Stir in the flour and cook for 1 minute. Draw off the heat and add the milk gradually, stirring continuously. Bring to the boil and cook for 3 minutes. Season with salt and pepper. Meanwhile, cook the pasta shells in lots of boiling salted water for 10 minutes, or until tender but still firm. Rinse in hot water and drain well. Place in a warmed serving dish and pour over mushroom sauce. Serve immediately.

This page: Pasta Spirals with Peas and Tomatoes. Facing page: Pasta Shells with Mushroom Sauce (top) and Farfalle with Tomato Sauce (bottom).

Spaghetti Amatriciana

| PREPARATION TIME: 10 minutes |
| COOKING TIME: 20 minutes |
| SERVES: 4 people |

30ml/2 tbsps olive oil
1 onion, peeled and chopped finely
6 rashers bacon, rind removed, cut
*   into strips*
1 x 400g/14oz tin plum tomatoes,
*   drained, seeds removed, and*
*   chopped roughly*
1 red chilli, seeded and chopped finely
275g/10oz spaghetti
60g/2oz pecorino cheese, grated

Heat the oil in a pan. Add the onion and bacon and cook over a gentle heat until the onion is soft but not coloured. Drain off any surplus fat. Add the tomato and chilli and stir. Simmer gently for 5 minutes, stirring occasionally. Meanwhile, cook the spaghetti in lots of boiling salted water for about 10 minutes, or until tender but still firm. Drain and return to the pan. Add the sauce and stir through. Serve with grated pecorino cheese.

Penne with Spicy Chilli Sauce

| PREPARATION TIME: 15 minutes |
| COOKING TIME: 40 minutes |
| SERVES: 4 people |

15ml/1 tbsp olive oil
2 cloves garlic, crushed
1 onion, peeled and chopped
120g/4oz bacon, rind removed, and diced
1 x 400g/14oz tin plum tomatoes
2 red chillies, seeded and chopped finely
2 spring onions, chopped
60g/2oz pecorino cheese, grated
Salt and pepper
275g/10oz penne

GARNISH
4 spring onions. Cut into 5cm/2-inch strips. Keeping one end intact, cut lengthways into strips. Soak in chilled water until the flower has opened.

Chop the tomatoes, removing the seeds by straining the juice. Heat the oil in a

pan and fry the garlic, onion and bacon gently for 10 minutes. Add the tomato, chillies, chopped spring onions, half the cheese and salt and pepper to taste. Cook, uncovered, for 20 minutes. Ten minutes before the sauce is ready, cook the penne in lots of boiling water for 10 minutes, or until tender but still firm. Rinse under hot water and drain well. Put into a warmed serving dish and toss together with half the sauce.

Pour the remaining sauce on top and garnish with spring onion flowers and remaining cheese, if desired. Serve at once.

This page: Pasta Shells with Gorgonzola Cheese Sauce (top) and Spaghetti Amatriciana (bottom). Facing page: Spaghetti with Egg, Bacon and Mushroom (top) and Penne with Spicy Chilli Sauce (bottom)

Pasta Shells with Gorgonzola Cheese Sauce

PREPARATION TIME: 5 minutes

COOKING TIME: 15 minutes

SERVES: 4 people

175g/6oz gorgonzola cheese
60ml/4 tbsps milk
30g/1oz butter
3 tbsps double cream
Salt
275g/10oz pasta shells
Parmesan cheese, grated

Heat the gorgonzola, milk and butter gently, in a pan. Stir to a sauce with a wooden spoon. Stir in the cream, adding a little salt if necessary. Meanwhile, cook the pasta in plenty of boiling salted water for 10 minutes, or until 'al dente'. Drain, shaking the colander to remove the excess water. Add the pasta to the hot sauce and toss to coat well. Serve immediately with grated Parmesan cheese on the side.

Spaghetti with Egg, Bacon and Mushroom

PREPARATION TIME: 10 minutes

COOKING TIME: 15 minutes

SERVES: 4 people

60g/2oz butter or margarine
225g/8oz mushrooms, sliced
120g/4oz bacon, rind removed, and diced
275g/10oz spaghetti
Salt and pepper
2 eggs, hard-boiled and chopped finely
1 tbsp chopped parsley
60g/2oz Parmesan cheese, grated

Melt half the butter in a frying-pan. Add the mushrooms and bacon, and cook for 10 minutes over a moderate heat, until the bacon is crisp. Meanwhile, cook the spaghetti in lots of boiling salted water until tender but still firm – about 10 minutes. Drain. Return to the pan. Add the rest of the butter, salt and lots of freshly ground black pepper, and the mushroom and bacon. Toss together. Serve with the hard-boiled eggs sprinkled on top, and parsley if desired. Serve grated Parmesan cheese separately.

Tagliatelle with Butter and Cheese

PREPARATION TIME: 5 minutes

COOKING TIME: 15 minutes

SERVES: 4 people

275g/10oz tagliatelle – 90g/3¹/₂oz each
    yellow, green and red tagliatelle
90g/3oz butter
90ml/6 tbsps double cream
60g/2oz Parmesan cheese, grated
Salt and pepper

Cook the tagliatelle in a large pan of boiling salted water for 10 minutes, or until just tender. Drain. Meanwhile, put the butter and cream in a pan and stir over a low heat until the butter has melted. Remove from the heat, add half the grated cheese and salt and pepper to taste. Stir into the tagliatelle and serve immediately with the remaining cheese on top.

Pasta Shells with Walnuts and Cream Cheese

PREPARATION TIME: 5 minutes

COOKING TIME: 15 minutes

SERVES: 4 people

15ml/1 tbsp olive oil
1 clove garlic, crushed
1 tbsp oregano
30g/1oz butter or margarine
60ml/4 tbsps milk
120g/4oz cream cheese
120g/4oz walnuts, chopped very finely
    (keep a few aside to decorate)
Salt and pepper
275g/10oz pasta shells
60ml/4 tbsps cream
Parmesan cheese, grated

Heat the oil in a pan. Add the crushed garlic and oregano and cook for 1 minute. Add the butter, milk, cream cheese, chopped walnuts, and salt and pepper to taste. Stir, and leave to simmer gently for 5 minutes. Meanwhile, cook the pasta shells in plenty of boiling salted water for 10 minutes, or until shells are tender but still firm. Drain in a colander, shaking to remove any trapped water. Put into a warmed serving dish. Remove the sauce from the heat; add the cream, and stir. Pour over the shells, and toss to coat evenly. Garnish with walnut halves. Serve immediately with grated Parmesan cheese.

Tagliatelle with Butter and Cheese (left)
and Pasta Shells with Walnuts and
Cream Cheese (below).

Farfalle with Beef, Mushroom and Soured Cream

| PREPARATION TIME: 10 minutes |
| COOKING TIME: 15 minutes |
| SERVES: 4 people |

275g/10oz farfalle (pasta butterflies/bows)
225g/8oz fillet or rump steak, sliced
30g/1oz unsalted butter
1 onion, peeled and sliced
120g/4oz mushrooms, sliced
15g/½oz flour
50ml/2 fl oz soured cream
10 green olives, stoned and chopped
Salt and pepper
Chopped parsley, to garnish

With a very sharp knife, cut the meat into narrow, short strips. Heat half the butter and fry the meat over a high heat until well browned. Set aside. Heat the remaining butter in a pan and gently fry the onion until soft and just beginning to colour. Add the mushrooms and cook for 3 minutes. Stir in the flour and continue frying for a further 3 minutes. Gradually stir in the soured cream, retaining a little for garnish. When fully incorporated, add the meat, olives and salt and pepper to taste. Meanwhile, cook the farfalle in plenty of boiling salted water for 10 minutes, or until tender but still firm. Drain well. Serve with the beef and mushroom sauce on top. Garnish with a little extra soured cream and chopped parsley.

Tortiglioni alla Puttanesca

| PREPARATION TIME: 10 minutes |
| COOKING TIME: 15 minutes |
| SERVES: 4 people |

1 x 200g/7oz tin plum tomatoes, drained
1 x 45g/1½oz tin anchovy fillets, drained
275g/10oz tortiglioni, spiral pasta
30ml/2 tbsps olive oil
2 cloves garlic, crushed
Pinch chilli powder
½ tsp basil
2 tbsps chopped parsley

This page: Tortiglioni alla Puttanesca. Facing page: Farfalle with Beef, Mushroom and Cream (top), Tagliatelle Carbonara (centre) and Pasta Spirals with Spinach and Bacon (bottom).

120g/4oz black olives, stoned and chopped
Salt and pepper

Chop the tomatoes and remove the seeds; chop the anchovies. Cook the pasta in plenty of boiling salted water for 10 minutes, or until tender but still firm. Rinse in hot water and drain. Pour into a warmed bowl. Meanwhile, heat the oil in a pan, add the garlic, chilli powder and basil and cook for 1 minute. Add the tomatoes, parsley, olives and anchovies, and cook for a few minutes. Season with salt and pepper. Pour the sauce over the pasta and mix together thoroughly. Serve immediately.

Pasta Spirals with Spinach and Bacon

| PREPARATION TIME: 15 minutes |
| COOKING TIME: 15 minutes |
| SERVES: 4 people |

½ small red pepper
1 small onion
90g/3oz bacon
1 small red chilli
275g/10oz pasta spirals
45ml/3 tbsps olive oil
1 clove garlic, crushed
225g/8oz spinach
Salt and pepper

Wash the spinach, remove the stalks and cut into thin shreds. Core and seed the pepper and slice half finely. Peel the onion and chop finely. Remove the rind from the bacon and chop; remove the seeds from the

chilli and slice thinly. Cook the pasta spirals in plenty of boiling salted water for 10 minutes, or until 'al dente'. Drain. Meanwhile, heat the oil in a pan and add the garlic, onion, bacon, chilli and red pepper. Fry for 2 minutes, add the spinach and fry for a further 2 minutes, stirring continuously. Season with salt and pepper to taste. Toss with pasta spirals. Serve immediately.

Tagliatelle Carbonara

PREPARATION TIME:	10 minutes
COOKING TIME:	15 minutes
SERVES:	4 people

1 tbsp olive oil
8 rashers bacon, chopped
Pinch of paprika
90ml/3 fl oz cream
2 eggs
30g/1oz Parmesan cheese, grated
275g/10oz tagliatelle
30g/1oz butter or margarine
Salt and pepper

Heat the oil in a frying pan, add the bacon and cook over a moderate heat until beginning to brown. Add the paprika and cook for 1 minute, then stir in the cream. Beat together the eggs and grated cheese. Meanwhile, cook the tagliatelle in lots of boiling salted water for 10 minutes, or until 'al dente'. Drain, return to the pan with the butter and black pepper and toss. Add the bacon mixture and the egg mixture and toss together well. Add salt to taste. Serve immediately.

Tagliatelle with Creamy Liver Sauce

PREPARATION TIME:	10 minutes
COOKING TIME:	15 minutes
SERVES:	4 people

60ml/4 tbsps olive oil
2 medium onions, peeled and sliced
1 clove garlic, crushed
120g/4oz mushrooms, sliced
460g/1lb chicken livers, cleaned and sliced
120ml/4 fl oz single cream
2 eggs, beaten
Salt and pepper

275g/10oz tagliatelle
1 tbsp chopped parsley

In a large frying pan, cook the onions and garlic gently in oil until softened. Add the mushrooms and cook for 3 minutes. Add the chicken livers to the onions and mushrooms and cook until lightly browned. Remove from the heat and stir in the cream. Return to a low heat and cook, uncovered, for a further 2 minutes. Remove from the heat, and stir in the lightly beaten eggs. Season with salt and pepper to taste. Meanwhile, cook the tagliatelle in plenty of boiling salted water for 10 minutes, or until tender but still firm, stirring occasionally. Drain the tagliatelle. Toss in oil and black pepper. Serve the sauce over the tagliatelle and sprinkle with parsley.

Pasta Spirals with Kidneys in Marsala Sauce

PREPARATION TIME:	15 minutes
COOKING TIME:	30 minutes
SERVES:	4 people

225g/8oz lambs' kidneys
1 tbsp flour
Salt and pepper
60g/2oz butter or margarine
1 small onion, peeled and chopped finely
1 clove garlic, crushed
90g/3oz bacon, rind removed, and diced
120g/4oz button mushrooms, sliced
90ml/6 tbsps Marsala, or dry white wine
275g/10oz pasta spirals

Remove the skin, fat and hard core from the kidneys. Cut in half lengthways. Add salt and pepper to the flour and mix well. Coat the kidneys in the seasoned flour. Heat the butter in a pan; add the onion and garlic, and cook until soft and translucent. Add the kidneys and brown on both sides. Add the bacon and mushrooms and cook, stirring frequently, for 3 minutes. Add the wine and bring to the boil. Simmer gently for 15 minutes, or until the kidneys are tender. Adjust seasoning. Meanwhile, cook the pasta spirals in plenty of boiling salted water for 10 minutes, or until tender but still firm. Rinse in hot water and drain well.

Serve immediately, with kidney sauce on top.

Tagliatelle with Creamy Liver Sauce (above right) and Pasta Spirals with Kidneys in Marsala Sauce (right).

Spaghetti with Tomato, Salami and Green Olives

PREPARATION TIME: 15 minutes

COOKING TIME: 15 minutes

SERVES: 4 people

1 x 400g/14oz tin plum tomatoes
¹/₂ tbsp oregano
1 clove garlic, crushed
150g/5oz salami, sliced and shredded
200g/7oz green olives, stoned and chopped
Salt and freshly ground black pepper
275g/10oz spaghetti
30ml/2 tbsps olive oil
60g/2oz pecorino cheese, grated

This page: Spaghetti with Tomato, Salami and Green Olives. Facing page: Spaghetti Bolognese (top) and Pasta Spirals with Creamy Parsley Sauce (bottom).

Push the tomatoes through a sieve into a saucepan. Add the oregano, salami and olives and heat gently. Add salt and pepper to taste. Meanwhile, cook the spaghetti in plenty of boiling salted water for 10 minutes, or until tender but still firm. Drain well. Heat the olive oil and freshly ground black pepper in the pan used to cook the spaghetti. Add spaghetti and pour the sauce over. Toss well. Serve with pecorino cheese.

Spaghetti Bolognese

PREPARATION TIME: 10 minutes

COOKING TIME: 1 hour 15 minutes

SERVES: 4 people

30g/1oz butter or margarine
1 tbsp olive oil
2 onions, finely chopped
1 carrot, scraped and chopped finely
225g/8oz minced beef
1 x 120g/4oz tin tomato purée
Salt and pepper
280ml/¹/₂ pint brown stock
2 tbsps sherry
275g/10oz spaghetti
Parmesan cheese, grated

Heat the butter and oil in a pan and sauté the onions and carrot slowly until soft. Increase the heat and add the minced beef. Fry for a few minutes, then stir, cooking until the meat is browned all over. Add the tomato purée, salt and pepper to taste and the stock, and simmer gently for about 45 minutes, stirring occasionally, until the mixture thickens. Add the sherry and cook for a further 5 minutes. Meanwhile, place the spaghetti in lots of boiling salted water and cook for 10 minutes, or until tender but still firm. Drain. Serve with the Bolognese sauce on top and sprinkle with Parmesan cheese.

Spaghetti with Sweetbread Carbonara

PREPARATION TIME: 10-15 minutes

COOKING TIME: 10 minutes

SERVES: 4 people

1 onion, chopped
3 tbsps olive oil
12oz wholewheat spaghetti
Salt and freshly ground black pepper to taste
225g/8oz calves' sweetbreads, blanched, skinned and chopped
6 tbsps dry white wine
4 eggs
60g/2oz grated Parmesan cheese
2 tbsps chopped fresh basil
1 clove garlic, peeled and crushed

Fry the onion gently in the olive oil for 5 minutes. Meanwhile, cook the spaghetti in a large pan of boiling, salted water for about 10 minutes, until just tender. Add the chopped sweetbreads to the onion and fry gently for 4 minutes. Add the white wine and cook briskly until it has almost evaporated. Beat the eggs with the Parmesan cheese, basil, garlic, and salt and pepper to taste. Drain the spaghetti thoroughly; immediately stir in the beaten egg mixture and the sweetbreads so that the heat from the spaghetti cooks the eggs. Garnish with basil and serve immediately.

Tortellini

PREPARATION TIME: 30 minutes

COOKING TIME: 15 minutes

SERVES: 4 people

DOUGH
275g/10oz strong plain flour
Pinch of salt
15ml/1 tbsp water
15ml/1 tbsp oil
3 eggs

FILLING
30g/1oz cream cheese
1 cooked chicken breast, finely diced
30g/1oz ham, finely diced
2 spinach leaves, stalks removed, cooked and chopped finely
1 tbsp grated Parmesan cheese
1 egg, beaten
Salt and pepper

SAUCE
300ml/½ pint single cream
60g/2oz mushrooms, cleaned and sliced
60g/2oz Parmesan cheese, grated
1 tbsp chopped parsley
Salt
Pepper

TO MAKE THE FILLING
Beat the cream cheese until soft and smooth. Add the chicken, ham, spinach and Parmesan cheese, and mix well. Add the egg gradually, and salt and pepper to taste. Set aside.

TO MAKE THE DOUGH
Sift the flour and salt onto a board. Make a well in the centre. Mix the water, oil and lightly beaten egg together and gradually pour into the well, working in the flour with the other hand, a little at a time. Continue until the mixture comes together in a firm ball of dough. Knead for 5 minutes, or until smooth and elastic. Put into a bowl, cover with a cloth and let stand for 5 minutes. Roll the dough out on a lightly floured board as thinly as possible. Using a 5cm/2-inch cutter, cut out rounds. Put ½ teaspoon of the filling into the centre of each round. Fold in half, pressing the edges together firmly. Wrap around fore-

finger and press ends together. Cook in batches in a large pan of boiling salted water for about 10 minutes until tender, stirring occasionally.

TO MAKE THE SAUCE
Meanwhile, gently heat the cream in a pan. Add the mushrooms, Parmesan cheese, parsley and salt and pepper to taste. Cook gently for 3 minutes.

Toss the sauce together with the tortellini. Serve immediately, sprinkled with parsley.

Chicken Liver Risotto with Red Beans

PREPARATION TIME: 15 minutes

COOKING TIME: about 28 minute

SERVES: 4 people

1 medium onion, finely chopped
2 tbsps olive oil
1 clove garlic, crushed
175g/6oz brown or wild rice
850ml/1½ pints chicken stock
Salt and freshly ground black pepper to taste
225g/8oz chicken livers, chopped
30g/1oz butter
175g/6oz cooked red kidney beans
1 tbsp chopped parsley

Fry the onion gently in the olive oil for 3 minutes. Add the garlic and the rice and stir over the heat for 1 minute, until the rice is evenly coated with oil. Gradually stir in the chicken stock. Bring to the boil and add salt and pepper to taste; cover and simmer for 40-50 minutes. Meanwhile, fry the chopped chicken livers in the butter for about 4 minutes until sealed on the outside but still pink in the centre. Drain the chicken livers with a slotted spoon and stir into the cooked rice together with the kidney beans and chopped parsley. Heat through. Serve hot with grated Parmesan cheese, if liked.

Facing page: Chicken Liver Risotto with Red Beans (top) and Spaghetti with Sweetbread Carbonara (bottom).

Spaghetti with Chicken Bolognese and Nuts

PREPARATION TIME: 15-20 minutes
COOKING TIME: 15 minutes
SERVES: 4 people

SAUCE
1 medium onion, finely chopped
1 clove garlic, peeled and finely chopped
2 tbsps olive oil
200ml/7 fl oz red wine
2 tbsps tomato purée
1 tbsp chopped fresh thyme
Salt and freshly ground black pepper to taste
225g/8oz finely chopped cooked chicken
6 tomatoes, skinned, seeded and chopped
1 tsp pesto sauce (see Noodles with Kidney Beans and Pesto recipe)
1 tbsp chopped cashew nuts
1 tbsp chopped walnuts

12oz spaghetti, plain or wholemeal

GARNISH
Chopped walnuts

Fry the onion and garlic in the olive oil for 3 minutes. Add the red wine, tomato purée, thyme and salt and pepper to taste. Bring to the boil and simmer for 10 minutes. Add the chopped chicken, chopped tomatoes, pesto sauce, cashew nuts and walnuts; simmer the sauce for a further few minutes. Meanwhile, cook the spaghetti in boiling, salted water for 8-10 minutes, until just tender. Drain the spaghetti thoroughly. If the sauce is too thick for your liking, thin it down with a little hot stock or water. Pile the cooked spaghetti into a serving dish and spoon the hot sauce over the top. Sprinkle with extra chopped walnuts and serve immediately.

Noodles with Kidney Beans and Pesto

PREPARATION TIME: 5 minutes
COOKING TIME: about 10 minutes
SERVES: 4 people

225g/8oz wholemeal or plain noodles
Salt and freshly ground black pepper to taste
1 small onion, finely chopped
2 tbsps olive oil
1 clove garlic, peeled and crushed
2 tsps pesto sauce
225g/8oz cooked red kidney beans

PESTO SAUCE
1 large bunch fresh basil
4 cloves garlic, crushed
3 tbsps pine kernels
150ml/5 fl oz good green olive oil
1 tbsp lemon juice
Salt and freshly ground black pepper to taste

GARNISH
Sprigs of fresh basil

TO MAKE THE SAUCE
Put all the ingredients into a food processor and blend until fairly smooth; the sauce should still have a little texture to it. Keep in an airtight container in the refrigerator for no more than a week. Serve with cooked pasta, with cold meats such as Italian ham, and with cooked game and poultry.

Cook the noodles in a large pan of boiling salted water until just tender. Meanwhile, fry the onion gently in the olive oil for 3 minutes; mix in the garlic and pesto sauce. Drain the cooked noodles thoroughly; add to the onion and pesto mixture, together with the red kidney beans. Stir over a gentle heat for 1-2 minutes and serve piping hot, garnished with basil.

This page: Spaghetti with Chicken Bolognese and Nuts. Facing page: Penne with Chilli Sauce (top) and Pasta with Tomato and Yogurt Sauce (bottom).

Pasta Spirals with Creamy Parsley Sauce

PREPARATION TIME: 5 minutes
COOKING TIME: 15 minutes
SERVES: 4 people

30g/1oz butter or margarine
15g/¹/₂oz flour
300ml/¹/₂ pint milk
275g/10oz pasta spirals
1 tbsp lemon juice, or 1 tsp vinegar
1 tbsp chopped parsley

Heat the butter in a pan; when melted, stir in the flour. Cook for 1 minute. Remove from the heat and gradually stir in the milk. Return to the heat and stir continuously until boiling. Cook for 2 minutes. Meanwhile, cook the pasta spirals in lots of boiling salted water for 10 minutes, or until tender but still firm. Rinse in hot water and drain well. Just before serving, add the lemon juice and parsley to the sauce and pour over pasta. Serve immediately.

Penne with Chilli sauce

PREPARATION TIME: 40 minutes
COOKING TIME: 20 minutes
SERVES: 4 people

275g/10oz pasta shells
1 clove garlic, crushed
1 onion, peeled and chopped
450g/1lb ripe tomatoes
1 aubergine
1 red chilli
2 tbsps oil
60g/2oz pecorino cheese, grated

Trim and cut aubergine into 1.5cm/ ¹/₂-inch slices and salt lightly. Leave for 30 minutes. Rinse and wipe dry with absorbent paper. Meanwhile, heat oil in a frying pan over a moderate heat and fry the onion and garlic until lightly coloured. Peel and seed the tomatoes and chop them roughly. Seed and finely chop the chilli. Cut the aubergine roughly and add to the onion. Fry together for five minutes, stirring occasionally. Add the tomatoes and chilli and mix well. Simmer the sauce gently, uncovered, for five minutes, stirring occasionally. Meanwhile, cook the pasta in plenty of boiling salted water for 10 minutes, or until tender but still firm. Rinse in hot water and drain well. Place in a warmed serving dish, add the hot sauce and toss well. Serve immediately with the pecorino cheese.

Noodles with Fresh Tomato Sauce

PREPARATION TIME: 10-15 minutes
COOKING TIME: 6-8 minutes
SERVES: 4 people

460g/1lb tomatoes, skinned and roughly chopped
1 small onion, peeled and chopped
1 clove garlic, peeled and chopped
1 tbsp chopped parsley
1 tbsp chopped basil
200ml/7 fl oz olive oil
Salt and freshly ground black pepper to taste
225g/8oz noodles (green, yellow or wholemeal)

GARNISH
Sprigs fresh basil

Put the tomatoes, onion, garlic, herbs, olive oil, and salt and pepper to taste into the blender and blend until smooth. Cook the noodles in boiling salted water until just tender. Drain thoroughly. Toss the cooked noodles in the prepared tomato sauce. Garnish with sprigs of fresh basil and serve immediately.

Pasta Shells with Agliata Sauce

PREPARATION TIME: 10 minutes
COOKING TIME: 8 minutes
SERVES: 4 people

275g/10oz wholemeal or plain pasta shells
Salt and freshly ground black pepper to taste

SAUCE
6 tbsps olive oil
3 tbsps coarsely chopped parsley
2 cloves garlic, peeled
1 tbsp pine kernels
1 tbsp blanched almonds

Cook the pasta shells in a large pan of boiling salted water until just tender. Meanwhile, make the sauce. Put all the ingredients into a blender and blend until smooth; add salt and pepper to taste. Drain the hot, cooked pasta shells and toss together with the prepared sauce. Serve immediately.

Pasta with Tomato and Yogurt Sauce

PREPARATION TIME: 5 minutes
COOKING TIME: 40 minutes
SERVES: 4 people

15g/¹/₂oz butter or margarine
15g/¹/₂oz flour
150ml/¹/₄ pint beef stock
1 x 400g/14oz tin plum tomatoes
1 bay leaf
Sprig of thyme
Parsley stalks
275g/10oz pasta shells
Salt and pepper
45ml/3 tbsps plain yogurt

Melt the butter in a pan. Stir in the flour, and pour in the stock gradually. Add the undrained tomatoes, bay leaf, thyme and parsley stalks. Season with salt and pepper. Bring to the boil and simmer for 30 minutes. Strain and push through a sieve, adjust seasoning, and reheat. Meanwhile, cook the pasta in plenty of boiling salted water for 10 minutes, or until tender but still firm. Rinse in hot water and drain well. Place in a warmed serving dish; pour over tomato sauce, then the yogurt. (Yogurt may be marbled through the tomato sauce.) Serve immediately.

Facing page: Pasta Shells with Agliata Sauce (top) and Baked Caponata and Noodles (bottom).

ITALIAN COOKING

BAKED & GRILLED DISHES

Baked Caponata and Noodles

PREPARATION TIME: 25-30 minutes

COOKING TIME: 35-40 minutes

OVEN TEMPERATURE:
190°C/375°F/Gas Mark 5

SERVES: 4 people

1 medium onion, thinly sliced
2 tbsps olive oil
2 cloves garlic, peeled and finely chopped
1 large green pepper, seeded and cut into cubes
1 large red pepper, seeded and cut into cubes
1 medium aubergine, cubed
6 tomatoes, skinned, seeded and chopped
1 tbsp tomato purée
3 tbsps red wine
Salt and freshly ground black pepper to taste
120g/4oz green noodles, cooked
90g/3oz grated cheese

Fry the onion gently in the olive oil for 4 minutes; add the garlic, red and green peppers, aubergine and chopped tomatoes and cook, covered, for 5 minutes. Add the tomato purée, wine and salt and pepper to taste. Simmer gently for 10-15 minutes, until the vegetables are almost soft. Remove from the heat and stir in the cooked noodles. Spoon into a shallow flameproof dish and sprinkle with the grated cheese. Bake in the oven for 15 minutes (alternatively, the dish can be flashed under a preheated grill).

This page: Macaroni Cheese with Anchovies. Facing page: Macaroni with Creamy Chicken Sauce (top) and Italian Casserole (bottom).

Macaroni Cheese with Anchovies

PREPARATION TIME: 5 minutes	
COOKING TIME: 15 minutes	
SERVES: 4 people	

225g/8oz macaroni
60g/2oz butter or margarine
60g/2oz flour
600ml/1 pint milk
½ tsp dry mustard
60g/2oz tin anchovy fillets
175g/6oz fontina cheese, grated
Salt and pepper

Drain the anchovies, and set enough aside to slice into a thin lattice over the dish. Chop the rest finely. Cook the macaroni in plenty of boiling salted water for 10 minutes, or until tender but still firm. Rinse in hot water and drain well. Meanwhile, melt the butter in a pan. Stir in the flour and cook for 1 minute. Remove from the heat and gradually stir in the milk. Return to the heat and bring to the boil. Simmer for 3 minutes, stirring continuously. Stir in the mustard, anchovies, and half the cheese. Season with salt and pepper to taste. Stir in the macaroni and pour into an ovenproof dish. Sprinkle with the remaining cheese over the top and make a latticework with the remaining anchovies. Brown under a hot grill. Serve immediately.

Macaroni with Creamy Chicken Sauce

PREPARATION TIME: 5 minutes	
COOKING TIME: 20 minutes	
SERVES: 4 people	

15ml/1 tbsp olive oil
120g/4oz chicken breasts
225g/8oz macaroni
60g/2oz butter
30g/1oz flour
600ml/1 pint milk
Salt and pepper
120g/4oz Mozzarella cheese, grated

Heat the oil in a frying pan and gently fry the chicken for 10 minutes,

or until cooked through. When cool, shred the chicken. Cook the macaroni in plenty of boiling salted water for 10 minutes, or until 'al dente'. Rinse in hot water. Drain well. Meanwhile, heat the butter in a pan, stir in the flour and cook for 1 minute. Draw off the heat and gradually add the milk, stirring all the time. Bring the sauce to the boil, stirring continuously, and cook for 3 minutes. Add the chicken, macaroni, and salt and pepper to taste, and mix well. Pour the mixture into an ovenproof dish and sprinkle with cheese. Cook under a preheated grill until golden brown.

Italian Casserole

PREPARATION TIME: 15 minutes	
COOKING TIME: 40 minutes	
OVEN TEMPERATURE: 180°C/350°F/Gas Mark 4	
SERVES: 4 people	

90g/3oz small macaroni
60g/2oz butter or margarine
1 onion, peeled and chopped
1 clove garlic, crushed
2 x 400g/14oz tins plum tomatoes
1 tbsp tomato purée
1 red pepper, cored, seeded and chopped
1 green pepper, cored, seeded and chopped
225g/8oz salami, cut into chunks
10 black olives, halved and stones removed
Salt and pepper
120g/4oz Mozzarella cheese, sliced thinly

Cook the macaroni in plenty of boiling salted water for 10 minutes, or until tender but still firm. Rinse under hot water and drain well. Place in a shallow, ovenproof dish. Meanwhile, heat the butter in a pan and fry the onion and garlic gently until soft. Add the undrained tomatoes, tomato purée, red and green peppers, salami and olives and stir well. Simmer, uncovered, for 5 minutes. Season with salt and pepper. Pour over the macaroni, stir and cover with the sliced cheese. Bake uncovered in a moderate oven for 20 minutes, until cheese has melted.

Pasta al Forno (above right) and Macaroni Cheese with Frankfurters (right).

Macaroni Cheese with Frankfurters

PREPARATION TIME: 10 minutes

COOKING TIME: 20 minutes

SERVES: 4 people

8 Frankfurter sausages, or 400g/14oz
    tin hot-dog sausages
225g/8oz macaroni
60g/2oz butter or margarine
60g/2oz flour
570ml/1 pint milk
175g/6oz Cheddar cheese, grated
1 tsp dry mustard
Salt and pepper

GARNISH
1 pimento, cut into strips

Poach the Frankfurters for 5-8
minutes. Remove skins and, when
cold, cut into diagonal slices. (If using
hot-dog sausage, just cut as required).
Cook the macaroni in plenty of
boiling salted water for about 10
minutes, or until tender but still firm.
Rinse in hot water and drain well.
Meanwhile, melt the butter in a pan.
Stir in the flour and cook for 1
minute. Draw off the heat, and
gradually add milk, stirring all the
time. Bring to the boil, stirring
continuously, and cook for 3 minutes.
Add the sausages, grated cheese,
mustard and salt and pepper to taste.
Stir well. Add the macaroni; mix in
well. Pour the mixture into an
ovenproof dish and sprinkle the
remaining cheese over the top. Make
a lattice of pimento and cook under a
preheated grill until golden brown.
Serve immediately.

Pasta al Forno

PREPARATION TIME: 10 minutes

COOKING TIME: 1 hour

OVEN TEMPERATURE:
190°C/375°F/Gas Mark 5

SERVES: 4 people

225g/8oz macaroni
4 tbsps butter or margarine
60g/2oz Parmesan cheese, grated
Pinch of grated nutmeg
Salt and pepper
2 eggs, beaten
1 medium onion, peeled and chopped
1 clove garlic, crushed
460g/1lb minced beef
2 tbsps tomato purée
6 tbsps beef stock
2 tbsps chopped parsley
4 tbsps red wine
2 tbsps plain flour
150ml/5 fl oz milk

Preheat the oven. Cook the macaroni
in plenty of boiling salted water for
10 minutes, or until tender but still
firm. Rinse under hot water. Drain.
Put one-third of the butter in the pan
and return the macaroni to it. Add
half the cheese, nutmeg, and salt and
pepper to taste. Leave to cool. Mix in
half the beaten egg, and put aside.
Melt half of the remaining butter in a
pan, and fry the onion and garlic
gently until the onion is soft. Increase
the temperature, add the meat and fry
until browned. Add the tomato
purée, stock, parsley and wine, and
season with salt and pepper. Simmer
for 20 minutes. In a small pan, melt
the rest of the butter. Stir in the flour
and cook for 30 seconds. Remove
from the heat and stir in the milk.
Bring to the boil, stirring
continuously, until the sauce
thickens. Beat in the remaining egg
and season to taste. Spoon half the
macaroni into a serving dish and
cover with the meat sauce. Put on
another layer of macaroni and
smooth over. Pour over white sauce,
sprinkle with remaining cheese and
bake in the oven for 30 minutes, until
golden brown. Serve immediately.

Spinach Lasagne

PREPARATION TIME: 10 minutes

COOKING TIME: 30 minutes

OVEN TEMPERATURE:
200°C/400°F/Gas Mark 6

SERVES: 4 people

8 sheets green lasagne

SPINACH SAUCE
90g/3oz butter or margarine
90g/3oz flour
150ml/1/4 pint milk
300g/11oz pack of frozen spinach,
    thawed and chopped finely
Pinch of ground nutmeg
Salt and pepper

PARMESAN SAUCE
30g/1oz butter or margarine
30g/1oz flour
300ml/1/2 pint milk
1 tsp French mustard
90g/3oz Parmesan cheese, grated
Salt

TO MAKE THE SPINACH SAUCE
Heat the butter in a pan, stir in the
flour and cook for 30 seconds. Draw
off the heat, and stir in the milk
gradually. Return to the heat and
bring to the boil, stirring
continuously. Cook for 3 minutes.
Add the spinach, nutmeg, and salt
and pepper to taste. Set aside.

Cook the spinach lasagne in lots of
boiling salted water for 10 minutes, or
until tender. Rinse in cold water and
drain carefully. Dry on a clean cloth.

TO MAKE THE PARMESAN SAUCE
Heat the butter in a pan and stir in
the flour, cooking for 30 seconds.
Remove from the heat and stir in the
milk. Return to the heat, stirring
continuously, until boiling. Continue
stirring, and simmer for 3 minutes.
Draw off the heat and add the
mustard, two-thirds of the cheese and
salt to taste.

Grease an ovenproof baking dish.
Line the base with a layer of lasagne,
followed by some of the spinach
mixture and a layer of the cheese
sauce. Repeat the process, finishing
with a layer of lasagne and a covering
of cheese sauce. Sprinkle with the
remaining cheese. Bake in a hot oven
until golden on top. Serve immediately.

Facing page: Spinach Lasagne.

Cannelloni

PREPARATION TIME: 10 minutes
COOKING TIME: 1 hour
OVEN TEMPERATURE: 180°C/350°F/Gas Mark 4
SERVES: 4 people

12 cannelloni shells
2 tbsps Parmesan cheese, grated
15ml/1 tbsp oil

FILLING
15ml/1 tbsp olive oil
2 cloves garlic, crushed
1 onion, peeled and chopped
460g/1lb minced beef
1 tsp tomato purée
1/2 tsp basil
1/2 tsp oregano
225g/8oz packet frozen spinach, thawed
1 egg, lightly beaten
60ml/4 tbsps cream
Salt and pepper to taste

TOMATO SAUCE
15ml/1 tbsp olive oil
1 onion, peeled and chopped
1 clove garlic, crushed
1 x 400g/14oz tin plum tomatoes
2 tbsps tomato purée
Salt and pepper

BÉCHAMEL SAUCE
300ml/1/2 pint milk
1 slice of onion
3 peppercorns

1 small bay leaf
30g/1oz butter or margarine
30g/1oz flour
Salt and pepper

TO MAKE THE FILLING

Heat the oil in a pan and fry the garlic and onion gently until soft and transparent. Add the meat and cook, stirring continuously, until well browned. Drain off any fat. Add the tomato purée, basil and oregano and cook gently for 15 minutes. Add the spinach, egg, cream and salt and pepper to taste. Cook the cannelloni in a large pan of boiling salted water for 15-20 minutes, until tender. Rinse in hot water and drain. Fill carefully with the meat mixture, using a teaspoon or a piping bag with a wide, plain nozzle.

TO MAKE THE TOMATO SAUCE

Heat the oil in a pan. Add the onion and garlic and cook gently until transparent. Push the tomatoes through a sieve and add to the pan with the tomato purée and salt and pepper to taste. Bring to the boil and then simmer for 5 minutes. Set aside.

TO MAKE THE BÉCHAMEL SAUCE

Put the milk in a pan with the onion, peppercorns and bay leaf. Heat gently for 1 minute, taking care not to boil, and set aside to cool for 5 minutes. Strain. Melt the butter in a pan. Remove from the heat and stir in the flour. Gradually add cool milk and bring to the boil, stirring continuously, until the sauce thickens. Add the seasoning.

Spread the tomato sauce on the base of an ovenproof dish. Lay the cannelloni on top and cover with Béchamel sauce. Sprinkle with grated cheese and bake in a moderate oven for 30 minutes. Serve immediately.

This page: **Italian Pasta Pie.** Facing page: **Cannelloni with Tomato and Cheese** (top) and **Cannelloni** (bottom).

Cannelloni with Tomato and Cheese

PREPARATION TIME:	10 minutes
COOKING TIME:	40 minutes
OVEN TEMPERATURE:	
200°C/400°F/Gas Mark 6	
SERVES:	4 people

12 cannelloni shells

FILLING
1 x 400g/14oz tin plum tomatoes
120g/4oz ricotta cheese
1 tsp tomato purée
1 tsp oregano or basil
120g/4oz Parmesan cheese, grated
Salt and pepper

SAUCE
15ml/1 tbsp olive oil
1 onion, peeled and chopped
1 x 400g/14oz tin plum tomatoes
1 tbsp cornflour
Salt and pepper
1 tbsp grated Parmesan cheese

Cook the cannelloni shells in a large pan of boiling salted water for 15-20 minutes, until tender. Rinse in hot water and drain well.

TO MAKE THE FILLING

Chop the tomatoes and remove pips. Set the juice aside for the sauce. Beat the ricotta cheese until smooth. Add the tomato purée, oregano or basil and Parmesan cheese and beat well. Finally, stir in the chopped tomato and salt and pepper to taste. Fill the cannelloni shells with a teaspoon, or a piping bag with a wide, plain nozzle. Place in an ovenproof dish.

TO MAKE THE SAUCE

Heat the oil in a saucepan and cook onion gently until transparent. Push the tomatoes and their juice through a sieve into the saucepan. Slake the cornflour with the reserved tomato juice and add to the pan. Bring to the boil and cook for 3 minutes, stirring continuously. Add salt and pepper to taste. Pour over the cannelloni and sprinkle with cheese. Place in a hot oven or under a preheated grill for 10 minutes, until heated through. Serve immediately.

Lasagne Rolls

PREPARATION TIME: 5 minutes
COOKING TIME: 15 minutes
SERVES: 4 people

8 sheets of lasagne pasta
60g/2oz button mushrooms
225g/8oz chicken breast fillets
60g/2oz butter or margarine
60g/2oz Gruyère or Cheddar cheese, grated
30g/1oz flour
150ml/¹/₄ pint milk
2 tsps oil
Salt and pepper

Fill a large saucepan two-thirds full of boiling salted water and 2 teaspoons of oil. Bring to the boil. Add 1 sheet of lasagne; wait about 2 minutes and add another sheet. Only cook a few at a time. When tender, remove, rinse under cold water and leave to drain. Repeat until all the lasagne is cooked. Meanwhile, wash and slice the mushrooms and slice the chicken. Put half the butter in a small frying pan and fry the mushrooms and chicken. In a small saucepan, melt the rest of the butter. Add the flour and cook for a minute. Remove from the heat and add the milk. Mix well and bring to the boil. Cook for 3 minutes. Add the sauce to the chicken and mushrooms and half the cheese, mixing well. Add salt and pepper to taste. Spread out the lasagne and spread one-eighth of the mixture at one end of each sheet. Roll up each piece of lasagne and put into an ovenproof dish. Sprinkle with the remaining cheese and put under a preheated grill until golden brown. Serve immediately.

Italian Pasta Pie

PREPARATION TIME: 35 minutes
COOKING TIME: 1 hour 5 minutes
OVEN TEMPERATURE:
190°C/375°F/Gas Mark 5
SERVES: 6-8 people

600g/1¹/₄lbs puff pastry
460g/1lb fresh spinach, cooked and drained thoroughly
120g/4oz ricotta cheese
1 clove garlic, peeled and crushed
Salt and freshly ground black pepper to taste
Generous pinch ground nutmeg
120g/4oz pasta shapes, cooked until just tender
90g/3oz shelled mussels
1 egg, beaten
1 tbsp chopped fresh basil

TO GLAZE PASTRY
Beaten egg
Grated Parmesan cheese

Roll out ²/₃ of the puff pastry quite thinly and use to line the sides and base of a loose-bottomed 18cm/7-inch round cake tin; press the pastry carefully into the shape of the tin, avoiding any cracks or splits. Roll out the remaining pastry to a circle large enough to cover the top of the cake tin generously. Mix the spinach with the ricotta cheese, garlic, salt, pepper and nutmeg to taste, cooked pasta, mussels and the beaten egg; spoon the filling into the pastry-lined pan. Brush the rim of the pastry with the beaten egg; lay the rolled-out portion of pastry over the filling and press the adjoining pastry edges together to seal. Trim off the excess pastry and pinch the edges decoratively. Cut decorative shapes from the pastry trimmings and fix on top of the pie. Glaze with beaten egg and sprinkle with grated Parmesan cheese. Bake in the oven for 45 minutes; cover with a piece of foil and cook for a further 20 minutes. Unmould carefully from the pan and serve the pie hot, cut into wedges. Note: the top of the pie can be sprinkled with a few pine kernels prior to baking, if desired.

Lasagne

PREPARATION TIME: 10 minutes
COOKING TIME: 45 minutes
OVEN TEMPERATURE:
200°C/400°F/Gas Mark 6
SERVES: 4 people

8 sheet lasagne

MEAT SAUCE
60g/2oz butter or margarine
1 onion, diced
1 stick celery, diced
1 carrot, diced
120g/4oz minced beef
1 tbsp flour
1 tbsp tomato purée
140ml/¹/₄ pint beef stock
1 tsp marjoram
Salt and pepper

BÉCHAMEL SAUCE
280ml/¹/₂ pint milk
6 black peppercorns
Slice of onion
1 bay leaf
Parsley stalks
60g/2oz butter or margarine
45g/1¹/₂ oz flour

TO MAKE THE MEAT SAUCE
Heat the butter in a pan and add the onion, celery and carrot. Sauté until the onion is golden. Add the minced beef and brown well. Stir in the flour; add the tomato purée, beef stock, marjoram and salt and pepper. Cook for 15 minutes. Meanwhile, cook the lasagne in lots of boiling salted water for 10 minutes, or until tender. Rinse in cold water and drain carefully. Lay out on a clean cloth to dry.

TO MAKE THE BÉCHAMEL SAUCE
Scald the milk in a saucepan with the peppercorns, slice of onion, bay leaf and parsley stalks and remove from the heat. Allow to cool for 5 minutes, then strain. Melt the butter in a saucepan. Stir in the flour and cook for 30 seconds. Remove from the heat and gradually add the milk, stirring continuously. Bring to the boil, then simmer for 3 minutes. Grease an ovenproof baking dish. Line the base with a layer of lasagne. Cover with a layer of meat sauce and a layer of Béchamel sauce. Place another layer of lasagne, repeating until all the ingredients are used, finishing with a layer of lasagne and a layer of Béchamel sauce. Bake in a preheated oven for about 20 minutes, or until the top is golden. Serve immediately.

Facing page: Lasagne Rolls (top) and Lasagne (bottom).

90g/3oz mushrooms, cleaned and
   chopped
1 stick celery, chopped
1 tbsp flour
150ml/¹/4 pint milk
4 tbsps cream
4 tbsps mayonnaise
1 tsp ground oregano
1 x 7oz tin tuna
Salt and pepper
3 shallots, peeled and chopped
1 egg, lightly beaten

TOPPING
4 tbsps breadcrumbs
60g/2oz cheese, grated
2 tbsps butter or margarine

Cook the cannelloni shells in a large pan of boiling salted water for 15-20 minutes until tender. Rinse in hot water and drain well. Meanwhile, melt the butter in saucepan. Fry the onion until transparent, add mushrooms and celery and fry for 5 minutes. Add the flour and fry until light golden brown. Draw off the heat and gradually add milk, stirring continuously. Return to the heat and bring to the boil. Cook for 3 minutes, stirring all the time. Add the cream, mayonnaise, oregano and undrained flaked tuna. Season with salt and pepper and stir until the sauce boils. Simmer for 3 minutes. Add shallots and egg, and mix well. Spoon the mixture into the cannelloni shells and place in an ovenproof dish. Sprinkle over a mixture of breadcrumbs and cheese and dot with butter or margarine. Bake in a moderate oven for 20 minutes. Serve immediately.

Spinach Crespelle

PREPARATION TIME:	45 minutes
COOKING TIME:	30 minutes
SERVES:	4 people

12 CRESPELLE
90g/3oz flour
Pinch of salt
3 eggs
225ml/8 fl oz water
2 tsps olive oil

30g/1oz butter or margarine, melted

FILLING
225g/8oz packet frozen spinach, thawed
225g/8oz cream cheese
30ml/2 tbsps cream
¹/2 tsp grated nutmeg
Salt and pepper
60g/2oz Parmesan cheese, grated
30g/1oz butter or margarine

TO MAKE THE CRESPELLE
Sift the flour with a pinch of salt. Break eggs into a bowl and whisk. Add the flour gradually, whisking all the time until the mixture is smooth. Stir in the water and mix the oil in well. Cover the bowl with a damp cloth and leave in a cool place for 30 minutes. Heat a crêpe pan or an 18cm/7-inch frying pan. Grease lightly with the melted butter and put a good tablespoon of batter in the centre. Tilt the pan to coat the surface evenly. Fry until the crespelle is brown on the underside. Loosen the edge with a palette knife; turn over and brown on the other side. Stack and wrap in a clean cloth until needed.

TO MAKE THE FILLING
Cook the spinach for 3 minutes in a pan of boiling water. Drain, chop and set aside. Beat the cream cheese and cream together until smooth. Add the nutmeg, half the cheese and salt and pepper to taste and mix in well. Mix the spinach into the cream cheese mixture. Divide equally between 12 crespelle, placing the mixture at one end and rolling up. Place in an ovenproof dish and dot with butter. Sprinkle with Parmesan cheese and place under a hot grill for 5 minutes, or until lightly browned on top. Serve immediately.

Crab Cannelloni

PREPARATION TIME:	10 minutes
COOKING TIME:	40 minutes
OVEN TEMPERATURE:	
200°C/400°F/Gas Mark 6	
SERVES:	4 people

12 cannelloni shells

FILLING
30g/1oz butter or margarine
3 shallots, chopped
225g/8oz crabmeat
¹/2 tsp Worcestershire sauce
1 tsp Dijon mustard
Salt and pepper

MORNAY SAUCE
30g/1oz butter or margarine
2 tbsps flour
280ml/¹/2 pint milk
30g/1oz Parmesan cheese, grated
Salt and pepper

Cook the cannelloni shells in a large pan of boiling salted water for 15-20 minutes, or until 'al dente'. Rinse in hot water and drain well. Meanwhile, heat the butter for the filling in a pan. Add the shallots, crabmeat, Worcestershire sauce, mustard and salt and pepper. Stir until heated through. Fill the cannelloni shells with the crab mixture using a piping bag fitted with a wide, plain nozzle. Place in a warmed ovenproof dish.

TO MAKE SAUCE
Heat the butter in a pan and stir in the flour. Remove from the heat and gradually add the milk. Return to the heat and bring to the boil; cook for 3 minutes, stirring continuously. Stir in half the cheese until it melts. Do not reboil. Season with salt and pepper. Pour over the cannelloni and sprinkle with the remaining cheese. Place in a preheated oven at 200°C/400°F/Gas Mark 6 for 10-15 minutes, or under a hot grill until golden brown. Serve immediately.

Facing page: Crespelle with Bolognese Sauce Filling (top) and Spinach Crespelle (bottom).

Crespelle with Tuna (left) and Crespelle with Chicken and Tongue (below).

Crespelle with Bolognese Sauce Filling

PREPARATION TIME: 45 minutes

COOKING TIME: 1 hour 15 minutes

SERVES: 4 people

12 CRESPELLE
90g/3oz flour
Pinch of salt
3 eggs
225ml/8 fl oz water
2 tsps olive oil
30g/1oz butter or margarine, melted

BOLOGNESE SAUCE
30g/1oz butter or margarine
15ml/1 tbps olive oil
2 onions, peeled and chopped finely
1 carrot, scraped and finely chopped
225g/8oz minced beef
120g/4oz tin tomato purée
300ml/1/2 pint brown stock
Salt and pepper
30ml/2 tbsps sherry

TOMATO SAUCE
15g/1/2oz butter
1 clove garlic, crushed
1/2 tsp basil
1 onion, peeled and chopped
1 x 400g/14oz tin plum tomatoes
Salt and pepper

TO MAKE THE BOLOGNESE SAUCE
Heat the butter and oil in a pan and fry the onions and carrot slowly until soft. Increase the heat and add the minced beef. Fry for a few minutes, then stir, cooking until meat is browned all over. Add the tomato purée, stock and salt and pepper to taste and simmer gently for about 3/4 hour, until the mixture thickens, stirring occasionally. Add 2 tbsps sherry and cook for a further 5 minutes.

TO MAKE THE CRESPELLE
Sift the flour with a pinch of salt. Break eggs into a bowl and whisk. Add the flour gradually, whisking all the time, until the mixture is smooth. Stir in the water and mix the oil in well. Cover the bowl with a damp cloth and leave in a cool place for 30 minutes. Heat a crêpe pan or an 18cm/7-inch frying pan. Grease lightly with the melted butter and put a good tablespoon of batter in the centre. Tilt the pan to coat the surface evenly. Fry until the crespelle is brown on the underside. Loosen the edge with a palette knife; turn over and brown on the other side. Stack and wrap in a clean cloth until needed.

TO MAKE THE TOMATO SAUCE
Heat the butter in a pan, and gently fry the garlic and basil for 30 seconds. Add the onion and fry until transparent. Add the tomatoes and cook for 10 minutes. Push through a sieve and return to the pan. Add salt and freshly ground black pepper to taste.

Lay crespelle out and put 2 heaped tablespoons of the Bolognese sauce filling at one end of each. Roll up and place in an ovenproof dish. Repeat until all crespelle have been filled. Put into a hot oven or under a preheated grill for 5 minutes. Reheat tomato sauce and pour over just before serving. Serve immediately.

Crespelle with Tuna

PREPARATION TIME: 40 minutes

COOKING TIME: 30 minutes

SERVES: 4 people

12 CRESPELLE
90g/3oz flour
Pinch of salt
3 eggs
225ml/8 fl oz water
2 tsps olive oil
30g/1oz butter or margarine, melted

TOMATO SAUCE
15g/1/2 oz butter or margarine
1 clove garlic, crushed
1/2 tsp basil
1 onion, chopped
1 x 400g/14oz tin tomatoes chopped
Salt and pepper
2 tbsps chopped parsley

FILLING
270g/9oz tin tuna, drained
3 tbsps mayonnaise
1 tbsp tomato purée

TO MAKE THE CRESPELLE
Sift the flour with a pinch of salt. Break eggs into a bowl and whisk. Add the flour gradually, whisking all the time until the mixture is smooth. Stir in the water and mix the oil in well. Cover the bowl with a damp cloth and leave in a cool place for 30 minutes. Heat a crêpe pan or an 18cm/7-inch frying pan. Grease lightly with the melted butter and put a good tablespoon of batter in the centre. Tilt the pan to coat the surface evenly. Fry until the crespelle is brown on the underside. Loosen the edge with a palette knife; turn over and brown on the other side. Stack and wrap in a clean cloth until needed.

TO MAKE THE SAUCE
Melt the butter in a pan and gently

fry the garlic and basil for 30 seconds. Add the onion and sauté until transparent. Add the tomato sauce and cook for 10 minutes. Push through a sieve and return to the pan. Add salt, freshly ground black pepper to taste and the parsley.

TO MAKE THE FILLING
Flake the tuna fish and put into a bowl. Mix together the mayonnaise and tomato purée and stir into the tuna. Divide the mixture equally between the crespelle, placing the mixture at one end and rolling up. Place in an ovenproof dish, pour over the tomato sauce and cook under a preheated grill for 5 minutes. Serve immediately.

Chicken and Ham Crêpes

PREPARATION TIME: 5 minutes	
COOKING TIME: 30 minutes	
OVEN TEMPERATURE: 200°C/400°F/Gas Mark 6	
SERVES: 4-6 people	

CRÊPE BATTER
120g/4oz flour
Pinch of salt
2 medium eggs
280ml/1/2 pint milk
1 tbsp olive oil
Oil to grease pan

FILLING
4 tbsps butter
3 tbsps flour
280ml/1/2 pint milk
2 tbsps grated fontina cheese
2 chicken breasts, cooked and shredded
2 slices cooked prosciutto, shredded
Salt and pepper

GARNISH
Parsley

Sift the flour and salt into a bowl. Make a well in the centre and drop in the eggs. Start to mix in the eggs gradually, taking in flour from around edges. When becoming stiff, add a little milk until all the flour has been incorporated. Beat to a smooth batter, then add the remaining milk. Stir in

the oil. Cover the bowl and leave in a cool place for 30 minutes. Heat a small frying pan, or 7-inch crêpe pan. Wipe over with oil. When hot, add enough batter mixture to cover the base of pan when rolled. Pour off any excess batter. When brown on the underside, loosen and turn over with a spatula and brown on the other side. Pile on a plate and cover with a clean towel until needed.

To make the filling, melt the butter in a pan. Stir in the flour and cook for 1 minute. Remove from the heat and gradually stir in the milk. Return to the heat, bring to the boil and cook for 3 minutes, stirring continuously. Add the cheese, chicken, prosciutto, salt and pepper and stir until heated through. Do not reboil. Divide the mixture evenly between the pancakes and roll up or fold into triangles. Place in a baking dish and cover with aluminium foil. Heat in a hot oven for 10 minutes. Garnish with parsley. Serve immediately.

Crespelle with Chicken and Tongue

PREPARATION TIME: 40 minutes	
COOKING TIME: 20 minutes	
OVEN TEMPERATURE: 230°C/450°F/Gas Mark 8	
SERVES: 4 people	

12 CRESPELLE
90g/3oz flour
Pinch of salt
3 eggs
225ml/8 fl oz water
2 tsps olive oil
30g/1oz butter or margarine, melted

BÉCHAMEL SAUCE
280ml/1/2 pint milk
4 peppercorns
1 bay leaf
Slice of onion
2 tbsps butter or margarine
1 tbsp flour
Salt and pepper

FILLING
225g/8oz chicken, cooked and shredded
225g/8oz tongue, cut into strips

TO MAKE THE CRESPELLE
Sift the flour with a pinch of salt. Break eggs into a bowl and whisk. Add the flour gradually, whisking all the time until the mixture is smooth. Stir in the water and mix the oil in well. Cover the bowl with a damp cloth and leave in a cool place for 30 minutes. Heat a crêpe pan or an 18cm/7-inch frying pan. Grease lightly with the melted butter and put a good tablespoon of batter in the centre. Tilt the pan to coat the surface evenly. Fry until the crespelle is brown on the underside. Loosen the edge with a palette knife; turn over and brown on the other side. Stack and wrap in a clean cloth until needed.

TO MAKE THE BÉCHAMEL SAUCE
Warm the milk with peppercorns, bay leaf and slice of onion. Remove from the heat and let stand for 5 minutes. Strain. Heat the butter in a pan. Stir in the flour and cook for 1 minute. Remove from the heat and gradually stir in two-thirds of the milk. Return to the heat and stir continuously until boiling. Simmer for 3 minutes. Add salt and pepper to taste.

Put half of the sauce in a bowl and add the chicken and tongue. Mix together. Beat the remaining milk into the remaining sauce.

Lay 1 crespelle on a plate and top with a layer of chicken and tongue filling. Cover with another crespelle and continue, finishing with a crespelle. Pour over the sauce and bake in a preheated oven for 10 minutes. Serve immediately.

Seafood Crêpes

PREPARATION TIME: 45 minutes	
COOKING TIME: 20 minutes	
OVEN TEMPERATURE: 200°C/400°F/Gas Mark 6	
SERVES: 4-6 people	

CRÊPE BATTER

120g/4oz flour
Pinch of salt
2 medium eggs
280ml/¹/₂ pint milk
1 tbsp olive oil
Oil to grease pan

FILLING

120g/4oz prawns, peeled and deveined
2 scallops, cleaned and sliced
120g/4oz whitefish fillets
Squeeze of lemon juice
1 tbsp lemon juice
4 tbsps butter or margarine
8 spring onions, sliced
3 tbsps flour
280ml/¹/₂ pint milk
Salt and pepper

Sift the flour and salt into a bowl. Make a well in the centre and drop in the eggs. Start to mix in the eggs gradually, taking in flour around edges. When becoming stiff, add a little milk until all the flour has been incorporated. Beat to a smooth batter, then add the remaining milk. Stir in the oil. Cover the bowl and leave in a cool place for 30 minutes. Heat a crêpe pan or 18cm/7-inch frying pan. Wipe over with oil. When hot, add enough batter mixture to cover the base of the pan when rolled. When brown on the underside, loosen, turn over with a spatula and brown on the other side. Poach the seafood in water with a squeeze of lemon juice for 4 minutes or until cooked through. Melt the butter in a pan. Add the spring onions and cook for 3 minutes. Remove and set aside. Stir in the flour and cook for 1 minute. Remove from the heat and gradually stir in the milk. Return to the heat, bring to the boil and cook for 3 minutes, stirring continuously. Add the spring onions, seafood, lemon juice and salt and pepper and stir well until heated through. Do not reboil. Divide the mixture evenly between pancakes and roll up or fold into triangles. Place in a baking dish and cover with foil. Heat in a hot oven for 10 minutes.

Right: Chicken and Ham Crêpes (top) and Seafood Crêpes (bottom).

ITALIAN COOKING

FISH & SEAFOOD

Sardine and Tomato Gratinée

PREPARATION TIME: 20-25 minutes

COOKING TIME: 15 minutes

OVEN TEMPERATURE:
225°C/425°F/Gas Mark 8

SERVES: 4 people

1kg/2.2lbs large, fresh sardines
3 tbsps olive oil
2 leeks, cleaned and sliced
150ml/5 fl oz dry white wine
225g/8oz tomatoes
Salt and pepper
2 tbsps chopped fresh herbs
60g/2oz grated Parmesan cheese
60g/2oz dry breadcrumbs
4 anchovy fillets (optional)

Scale and clean the sardines. Heat the oil in a large frying pan, add the sardines and brown well on both sides. Remove from the pan and set aside. Add the leeks and cook slowly in the oil from the sardines. When they are soft, pour in the wine and boil to reduce by about two-thirds. Add the tomatoes, salt, pepper and herbs, and continue to simmer for 1 minute. Pour into an ovenproof dish and put the sardines on top. Sprinkle with the cheese and breadcrumbs. Bake for about 5 minutes. If desired, cut anchovy fillets lengthways into thinner strips and lay them on top of the gratinée before serving.

This page: Sardine and Tomato Gratinée. **Facing page:** Spaghetti Marinara (top) and Pasta Shells with Seafood (bottom).

Pasta Shells with Seafood

PREPARATION TIME: 5 minutes

COOKING TIME: 15 minutes

SERVES: 4 people

60g/2oz butter or margarine
2 cloves garlic, crushed
140ml/5 fl oz dry white wine
225ml/8 fl oz cream
1 tbsp cornflour
2 tbsps water
1 tbsp lemon juice
Salt and pepper
275g/10oz pasta shells
460g/1lb prawns, shelled and deveined
120g/4oz scallops, cleaned and sliced
1 tbsp chopped parsley

Melt the butter in a pan. Add the garlic, and cook for 1 minute. Add the wine and cream, bring back to the boil and cook for 2 minutes. Slake the cornflour with the water, and pour into the sauce. Stir until boiling. Add lemon juice and salt and pepper to taste. Meanwhile, cook the pasta in plenty of boiling salted water for about 10 minutes. Drain, shaking to remove the excess water. Add the prawns and scallops to the sauce and cook for 3 minutes. Pour the sauce over the pasta shells, toss, and garnish with parsley.

Spaghetti Marinara

PREPARATION TIME: 10 minutes

COOKING TIME: 20 minutes

SERVES: 4 people

75ml/5 tbsps water
75ml/5 tbsps dry white wine
1 bay leaf
4 peppercorns
225g/8oz scallops, cleaned and sliced
30ml/2 tbsps olive oil
2 cloves garlic, crushed
1 tsp basil
1 x 400g/14oz tin plum tomatoes, seeded and chopped
45g/1½oz tin anchovy fillets
1 tbsp tomato purée
275g/10oz spaghetti
460g/1lb prawns, shelled and deveined
1 tbsp chopped parsley
Salt and pepper

Drain the anchovies and cut into small pieces. Place the water, wine, bay leaf and peppercorns in a pan. Heat to a slow boil. Add the scallops and cook for 2 minutes. Remove and drain. Heat the oil, add the garlic and basil, and cook for 30 seconds. Add the tomatoes, anchovies and tomato purée. Stir until combined. Cook for 10 minutes. Meanwhile, cook the spaghetti in a large pan of boiling salted water for 10 minutes, or until tender but still firm. Drain. Add seafood to sauce and cook a for a further 1 minute. Add the parsley and stir through. Season with salt and pepper to taste. Toss gently. Pour the sauce over spaghetti and serve immediately, sprinkled with parsley.

Scampi Florentine

PREPARATION TIME: 15 minutes

COOKING TIME: 15-20 minutes

SERVES: 4 people

1kg/2.2lbs fresh spinach
60g/2oz butter
1 shallot
225g/8oz button mushrooms
2 tomatoes, seeds removed
Salt and pepper
Nutmeg
15g/½oz flour
300ml/½ pint milk
60g/2oz grated fontina cheese
460g/1lb cooked scampi

Rinse the spinach well, removing any thick stalks, and put into a saucepan with a good pinch of salt. Cover and cook for about 3-5 minutes. In a small saucepan, heat half the butter. Chop the shallot finely and cook it in the butter until soft. Wipe and slice the mushrooms and cook with the shallots. Drain the spinach well and chop finely. Mix the shallots, mushrooms and tomatoes with the spinach, add seasoning and a pinch of nutmeg, and put into an ovenproof dish. Melt half the remaining butter in a saucepan and add the flour. Gradually stir in the milk, return the sauce to the heat and bring to the boil. Season with salt and pepper. Grate the cheese and add half to the sauce. Shell the scampi if necessary.

Heat the remaining butter and quickly toss scampi in it over heat. Put the scampi on top of the spinach and cover with sauce. Sprinkle the remaining cheese over and brown quickly under a hot grill. Serve immediately.

Prawn Risotto

PREPARATION TIME: 15 minutes

COOKING TIME: 25 minutes

SERVES: 4 people

4 tomatoes
3 cloves garlic
1 large onion
460g/1lb unpeeled prawns
1 glass white wine

Below: Prawn Risotto. Facing page: Scampi Florentine (top) and Grilled Swordfish Steaks with Grapefruit (bottom).

3 tbsps olive oil
2 tbsps chopped parsley
175g/6oz round Italian or risotto rice
1 tsp tomato purée
Salt and pepper
2 tbsps grated Parmesan cheese

Skin, seed and chop the tomatoes and peel and chop the garlic and onion. Peel the prawns, leaving 4 unpeeled for garnish. Cook the wine and prawn shells together and leave to cool. Heat the olive oil in a fairly wide pan or sauté pan. Soften the onion in the oil without browning. Add the garlic and parsley. Fry gently for 1 minute. Add the rice and strain on the wine. Add the tomato purée and more water to barely cover the rice. Season with salt and pepper, stirring the rice and adding more water as it becomes absorbed. The rice will take about 20 minutes to cook. When it is cooked, toss in the peeled prawns and cheese to heat through. Pile risotto rice into a serving dish and top with unpeeled prawns. Sprinkle over some chopped parsley.

Grilled Swordfish Steaks with Grapefruit

PREPARATION TIME: 10 minutes

COOKING TIME: 10 minutes

SERVES: 4 people

4 swordfish steaks, 2.5cm/1-inch thick
60g/2oz melted butter
Coarsely ground pepper
2 grapefruit
1 tbsp caster sugar

Melt the butter and brush the fish steaks on both sides. Heat the grill to moderate. Season the steaks with coarsely ground pepper. Grill on one side for about 5 minutes, turn, brush again with butter, then grill for about 3 minutes. Slice one grapefruit thinly and peel and segment the other. Sprinkle the slices with caster sugar and brown under the grill. Put the segments on top of the fish and heat through for 1 minute. Overlap the grilled grapefruit slices on serving plates and put the fish on top.

Vermicelli Pescatore

PREPARATION TIME: 15 minutes

COOKING TIME: 40 minutes

SERVES: 4 people

120g/4oz mussels
120g/4oz cockles
225g/8oz cod fish fillets
120g/4oz squid, cleaned
60ml/4 tbsps olive oil
275g/10oz vermicelli
250ml/8 fl oz dry white wine
1 x 400g/14oz cans plum tomatoes
Half a green pepper, diced
4 large prawns
4 fresh oysters

Prepare the seafood. If using fresh mussels, clean closed mussels, removing beard, and cook in boiling water for 3 minutes until they open (discard any that remain closed). Cool and remove from shells, keeping a few in their shells for garnish if desired. Skin and bone the cod fillets and cut into 1.5cm/½-inch pieces. Clean the squid and cut into rings. Force tomatoes and their juice through a sieve and set aside. Heat 30ml/2 tbsps oil in a pan and add the squid. Fry gently until golden brown, then add wine, tomatoes, green pepper, and salt and pepper to taste. Simmer for 20 minutes then add the fish. Simmer for a further 10 minutes, stirring occasionally. Add cockles and mussels and, when mixture reboils, adjust seasoning. Meanwhile, cook the pasta in lots of boiling salted water for 10 minutes, or until tender but still firm. Drain well. Add seafood, and toss. Garnish with prawns and fresh oysters.

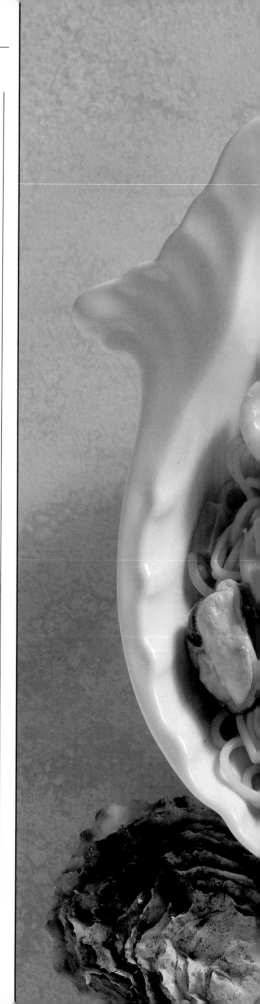

Right: Vermicelli Pescatore.

Fritto Misto Mare

PREPARATION TIME: 10 minutes

COOKING TIME: 5-6 minutes

SERVES: 4 people

460g/1lb whitebait, smelts or sprats, or
whitefish
225g/8oz uncooked scampi
120g/4oz scallops with roe attached
275ml/¹/₂ pint shelled mussels
Vegetable oil for deep frying
Salt

BATTER
275ml/¹/₂ pint water
2 tbsps olive oil
120g/4oz plain flour
Pinch salt

1 tsp ground nutmeg
1 tsp ground oregano
1 egg white

GARNISH
Parsley sprigs
1 lemon, cut into wedges

First make the batter so that it can
rest for ¹/₂ hour while the fish is being
prepared. Blend the oil with water,
and gradually stir into the flour sifted
with a pinch of salt. Beat the batter
until quite smooth and add the
nutmeg and oregano. Just before
using, fold in stiffly beaten egg white.
If using smelts or sprats, cut the heads
off the fish; if using whitefish, cut

into chunks about 2.5cm/1 inch thick.
Shell the scampi if necessary. If the
scallops are large, cut them in half.
Heat the oil to 190°C/375°F. Dip the
fish and shellfish, one at a time, into the
batter, allowing surplus batter to drip
off. Then put them into the frying basket
and into the hot oil. Fry for 5-6 minutes,
or until crisp and golden. Drain on
crumpled absorbent paper. Sprinkle
lightly with salt and garnish with parsley
sprigs and lemon wedges. If desired, a
tartare sauce may be served.

**This page: Fritto Misto Mare. Facing
page: Fish Stew (top) and Baked Sea
Bass with Fennel and Mixed Vegetables
(bottom).**

Fish Stew

PREPARATION TIME: about 15 minutes
COOKING TIME: about 35 minutes
SERVES: 4 people

1 medium onion, finely chopped
3 tbsps olive oil
2 cloves garlic, crushed
680g/1½lbs tomatoes, skinned, seeded and chopped
2 tbsps tomato purée
570ml/1 pint dry red wine
1.1 litres/2 pints mussels in their shells, scrubbed
8 king prawns
120g/4oz peeled prawns
4 crab claws, partly shelled
Salt and black pepper to taste

TO SERVE
8 small slices stale, crusty bread
A little olive oil
1 large clove garlic, crushed
Chopped parsley

Fry the onion gently in the olive oil for 3 minutes. Add the garlic and chopped tomatoes and fry gently for a further 3 minutes. Add the tomato purée and red wine and bring to the boil; simmer for 15 minutes. Add the mussels and simmer, covered, for 5 minutes. Add the king prawns, peeled prawns and crab claws, and simmer for a further 5 minutes. Meanwhile, prepare the bread croûtes. Brush the slices of bread with a little olive oil and rub with the garlic. Grill until crisp and golden and then sprinkle with chopped parsley. Spoon the fish stew into a deep serving dish and top with the bread croûtes. Serve immediately.

This page: Grilled Red Mullet with Garlic Sauce. Facing page: Egg and Fish Flan.

Baked Sea Bass with Fennel and Mixed Vegetables

PREPARATION TIME: 30 minutes
COOKING TIME: 35-40 minutes
OVEN TEMPERATURE: 190°C/375°F/Gas Mark 5
SERVES: 4-6 people

1 sea bass, about 1.15kg/2½lbs in weight, scaled, gutted and cleaned
Salt and freshly ground black pepper to taste
1 tbsp chopped fresh fennel
1 large clove garlic, peeled and finely chopped
Coarsely grated rind of ½ lemon
2 tbsps olive oil
4 tbsps dry white wine

MIXED VEGETABLES
2 large carrots, peeled and cut into thin strips
3 stalks celery, cut into thin strips
120g/4oz green beans

GARNISH
Feathery sprigs of fennel or dill

Season the sea bass inside and out; put the chopped fennel, garlic and lemon rind into the cavity of the fish. Lay the fish on a rectangle of greased foil sitting on a baking sheet; pinch up the edges of the foil. Brush the sea bass with olive oil and spoon over the dry white wine. Pinch the foil together over the fish completely to enclose it. Bake in the oven for 35-40 minutes – the foil can be folded back for the last 10 minutes of cooking time, if desired. For the vegetables, steam over gently simmering water for about 10 minutes – they should still be slightly crunchy. Arrange the cooked sea bass on a large, oval serving platter and surround with small "bundles" of the steamed vegetables. Garnish with sprigs of fennel.

Sole and Prawn with Lemon

PREPARATION TIME: 15 minutes

COOKING TIME: 10-15 minutes

SERVES: 4 people

225g/8oz prawns
2 large sole
Seasoned flour
90g/3oz butter
2 tbsps oil
Salt
Pepper
Lemon juice

GARNISH
Lemon slices

Peel the tails, shells and legs from 4 whole prawns and set aside. Fillet and skin the sole; rinse and dry well, and coat lightly in seasoned flour. Heat the oil in a large frying pan and add 30g/1oz of the butter. Lay in the fish fillets and cook quickly to brown both sides. Transfer them to a serving dish and keep warm. Briefly cook the remaining peeled prawns in the butter remaining in the pan and scatter them over the cooked fillets. Wipe out the pan, put in the remaining butter and cook to a good nut brown colour. Add a squeeze of lemon juice. Adjust seasoning, then pour over the sole and prawns. Garnish with whole prawns and lemon slices.

Tuna and Fennel

PREPARATION TIME: 15 minutes

COOKING TIME: 6-8 minutes

SERVES: 4 people

4 tuna steaks, cut 2.5cm/1 inch thick
1 clove garlic
4 tbsps olive oil
4 tbsps white wine
Crushed black pepper
Salt
1 head Florentine fennel

Peel the garlic and cut into thin slivers. Stick these into the tuna steaks with a sharp knife. Mix together the oil, wine and pepper and pour over steaks in a shallow dish. Leave to marinate in a refrigerator for 1 hour. Heat grill to high and grill fish for 3-4 minutes per side, basting frequently with the marinade. Reserve the green, feathery tops of the fennel. Cut the head in half and slice into 0.5cm/¼-inch pieces. Put into boiling salted water and cook for 5 minutes. Season and keep warm. Garnish the tuna steaks with reserved fennel top and serve with the cooked, sliced fennel.

Monkfish Piperade

PREPARATION TIME: 20 minutes

COOKING TIME: 30 minutes

OVEN TEMPERATURE:
180°C/350°F/Gas Mark 4

SERVES: 4 people

680g/1½lbs monkfish fillets
2 onions
2-3 tbsps olive oil
1 yellow pepper
1 red pepper
1 green pepper
1-2 cloves garlic
200ml/7oz tinned tomatoes
Salt and pepper
1 small French stick
Oil for deep frying

Slice the onions thinly and soften in 1 tbsp olive oil in a saucepan. Slice all the peppers in half, remove seeds, and cut into 1.25cm/½-inch strips.

This page: **Tuna and Fennel.** Facing page: **Sole and Prawn with Lemon** (top) and **Monkfish Piperade** (bottom).

Crush the garlic and add to the onions when tender, then cook gently for another 5 minutes. Add the tomatoes and seasoning and let sauce simmer until liquid has reduced by about half. If the fish fillets are large, cut them in half again lengthways. Heat the remaining oil in a saucepan and cook the fish until it is lightly brown. Transfer fish to an ovenproof dish and when the piperade is ready, spoon it over the top of the fillets. Heat through in the oven for about 10-15 minutes. Meanwhile, slice the French stick on the slant into 1.25cm/ ½-inch slices. Fry in enough oil to barely cover until golden brown, then drain on kitchen paper. Put the monkfish piperade into a serving dish and surround with the bread.

Buttered Perch

PREPARATION TIME: 10 minutes

COOKING TIME: 12-15 minutes

SERVES: 4 people

1kg/2¼lbs perch (or sole or other whitefish) fillets
Seasoned flour
2 eggs
Salt
Fine cornmeal
3 tbsps oil
120g/4oz butter
Lemon juice

GARNISH
Lemon wedges
Parsley sprigs

Skin, wash and dry the fish fillets well, then cut each lengthways into 4 strips and toss in seasoned flour. Beat the eggs, adding a pinch of salt, then coat the fish before tossing it in the cornmeal. Shake off the excess. Heat oil in a large frying pan and add 1 tbsp butter. Shallow-fry the fish briskly for about 5-6 minutes, frying in 2 or 3 batches. Drain on absorbent paper and keep warm. Melt the remaining butter and add lemon juice. Pour over the fish and serve with lemon wedges and sprigs of parsley.

Venetian Prawn Risotto

PREPARATION TIME: 15 minutes

COOKING TIME: 30 minutes

SERVES: 4 people

225g/8oz risotto or Italian rice
Good pinch saffron, or 1 packet saffron powder
60g/2oz butter
1 shallot, finely chopped
Salt and pepper
2 tbsps chopped parsley
1 medium onion
2 sticks celery
1 green pepper
1 red pepper
120g/4oz mushrooms
400ml/14oz tin tomatoes
1 bay leaf
½ tsp chopped thyme
1 tsp sugar
460g/1lb prawns

Rinse the rice, put into a large saucepan of boiling salted water and cook for about 12 minutes. Measure 3 tsps of the boiling water and soak the saffron in it. Melt half the butter and

cook the shallot. Butter a 600ml/1-pint ring mould well and set aside. Drain the rice when cooked and mix with the cooked shallot, seasoning, 1 tbsp chopped parsley and saffron liquid. Stir well and ensure rice is evenly coloured with the saffron. Put this mixture into the ring mould, pressing down well and leave to keep warm. Melt the remaining butter, chop the onion and celery finely, slice the peppers into fine shreds and slice the mushrooms. Cook the onion in the butter until just lightly coloured, then add peppers and mushrooms and cook gently for several minutes. Add the celery and tomatoes and bring to the boil. Reduce the heat and add the bay leaf, remaining parsley, thyme, sugar and seasoning. Allow to simmer for about 12 minutes, then add the prawns and heat through. Carefully unmould the rice ring onto a serving plate and pour the Venetian shrimp onto the centre.

This page: Buttered Perch. Facing page: Venetian Prawn Risotto.

Pizza Marinara

PREPARATION TIME: 15 minutes

COOKING TIME: 25-30 minutes

OVEN TEMPERATURE:
220°C/425°F/Gas Mark 7

SERVES: 4 people

145g/5oz flour, sifted
1 tsp baking powder
1/2 tsp salt
90ml/3 fl oz milk
2 tbsps salad oil
120g/4oz tinned tomatoes
1 tsp tomato purée
1/2 tsp oregano
1/2 tsp basil
Fennel seeds
Salt and pepper
1 clove garlic, crushed
30g/1oz prawns
30g/1oz cockles
6-8 mussels
4 anchovy fillets
2-3 black olives
1 tsp capers
120g/4oz sliced Mozzarella cheese

Sift the flour, baking powder and salt into a bowl and add milk and oil. Stir vigorously until the mixture leaves the sides of the bowl. Press it into a ball and knead it in the bowl for about 2 minutes, until smooth. Cover, and leave it to sit while preparing the sauce. Put the tomatoes, purée, herbs, seasoning and garlic together in a small saucepan. Bring to the boil and reduce to thicken. Leave to cool. Roll out the dough into a 24cm/12-inch circle. Spread the sauce over evenly, leaving a 1.25cm/1/2-inch border around the edge. Scatter over the shellfish, anchovy fillet, olives and capers. Slice the cheese thinly and place it on top of the fish. Bake in a preheated oven until the cheese browns lightly and the crust is crisp.

ITALIAN COOKING
MEAT & POULTRY

Veal Chops with Wine

PREPARATION TIME: 30 minutes

COOKING TIME: 1 hour 20 minutes

OVEN TEMPERATURE:
180°C/350°F/Gas Mark 4

4 veal chops
3 tbsps flour
Salt and pepper
2 tbsps oil
1 onion, chopped
120g/4oz small button mushrooms, left
   whole
225ml/8 fl oz white wine

Trim the chops and coat with some of
the flour and a little salt and pepper.
Heat the oil and brown the chops on
both sides, then transfer to a casserole
dish. Add the onion to the remaining
oil and cook until lightly browned.
Add the remaining flour and mix
well. Add the mushrooms and wine
and bring to the boil, stirring all the
time. Pour the sauce over the chops
in the casserole. Cover and cook in a
preheated oven for about 1 hour, or
until tender.

Veal Escalopes

PREPARATION TIME: 30 minutes

COOKING TIME: 15 minutes

SERVES: 4 people

4 thin slices veal, approx. 340g/12oz each
1 egg, beaten
6 tbsps white breadcrumbs
6 tbsps Parmesan cheese, finely grated
Salt and pepper
2 tbsps oil

4 tbsps butter

Trim the veal slices to give neat
shapes and dip them in the beaten
egg. Mix the breadcrumbs and grated
cheese together and season with salt
and pepper. Use this to coat the veal.

Fry the veal on both sides in hot oil
and butter for about 10 minutes, until
golden brown. Serve with vegetables.

**Facing page: Pizza Marinara. This page:
Veal Chops with Wine.**

of marjoram, bay leaf, carrots and celery, cover and allow to simmer for 45 minutes. Melt the butter in a small pan and stir in the flour. Cook until golden brown and pour in the stock from the veal. Cook until thickened and pour over the veal. Add the parsley and marjoram and adjust the seasoning. Stir in the olives and keep warm. Heat the oil in a frying pan. Cut the bread into triangles and fry until golden brown on both sides. Drain well and serve with the veal.

Veal Chops with Cheese

PREPARATION TIME: 35 minutes
COOKING TIME: 30 minute
OVEN TEMPERATURE:
190°C/375°F/Gas Mark 5
SERVES: 4 people

8 thick veal chops
120g/4oz butter
Salt and pepper
3 cups fontina cheese, grated
2 eggs
60ml/4 tbsps double cream
Grated nutmeg
120ml/4 fl oz white wine

Melt the butter in a large frying pan with an ovenproof handle. Add the veal chops and sear them on both sides over a high heat. Reduce the heat, season the chops, cover the pan and cook gently for about 20 minutes, turning the chops once. In a bowl mix together the cheese, eggs and cream. Season and add the nutmeg. Drain off the cooking butter from the pan and reserve it. Put some of the cheese mixture on each chop. Add the wine to the pan and place it, uncovered, in a preheated oven for 10 minutes to finish the cooking. Baste the chops with the reserved cooking butter once or twice.

Veal Rolls

PREPARATION TIME: 30 minutes
COOKING TIME: 2 hours 15 minutes
OVEN TEMPERATURE:
180°C/350°F/Gas Mark 4
SERVES: 4 people

4 veal escalopes
2 tbsps melted butter
Salt and pepper
1 small onion, finely chopped
Grated rind of 1 lemon
1 tbsp parsley, finely chopped

SAUCE
3 tbsps butter
1 small onion, grated and finely chopped
3 tbsps flour
225ml/8 fl oz chicken stock
225ml/8 fl oz white wine
1 small tin tomato purée
Salt and pepper

Brush the escalopes with a little butter and sprinkle with salt and pepper, onion, parsley, and lemon, and roll up tightly. Secure with a small skewer or thin string. Put into a casserole dish. To make the sauce, melt the butter, add the onion and sauté for a few minutes without browning. Stir in the flour and cook until lightly browned. Pour on the stock and wine. Add the tomato purée, salt and pepper and stir well. Pour sauce over the veal rolls and cook in the oven, covered, for 30-40 minutes or until veal is tender.

Veal Casserole

PREPARATION TIME: 30 minutes
COOKING TIME: 50 minutes
SERVES: 4 people

680g/1½lbs veal shoulder, cubed
Salt and pepper
225ml/8 fl oz chicken stock
1 sprig marjoram
1 bay leaf
2 large carrots
2 sticks celery, chopped
3 tbsps butter or margarine
3 tbsps flour
1 tbsp chopped parsley
½ tbsp chopped marjoram
10 stuffed green olives
4 slices of bread
4 tbsps oil

Season the veal. Bring the chicken stock to the boil, add the meat, sprig

This page: Veal Chops with Cheese (left) and Veal Chops with Mushrooms (right). Facing page: Veal Rolls (top), Veal Casserole (centre right) and Veal Escalopes (bottom).

Veal Chops with Mushrooms

PREPARATION TIME: 45 minutes

COOKING TIME: 1 hour 10 minutes

OVEN TEMPERATURE:
160°C/325°F/Gas Mark 3

SERVES: 4 people

4 veal chops
Salt and pepper
2 tbsps oil
4 medium-sized carrots, sliced
120g/4oz mushrooms
1 small onion, sliced
4 tbsps white wine
2 tomatoes, peeled and sliced

Trim the chops and season. Heat the oil and brown the chops on both sides, then transfer to a casserole dish. Add all the other ingredients and cook in a preheated oven for about 1 hour.

Veal Cutlets with Vegetables

PREPARATION TIME: 5 minutes

COOKING TIME: 30 minutes

SERVES: 4 people

60g/2oz clarified butter, or butter and oil
*   mixed*
90g/3oz button onions
4 veal cutlets
Salt and pepper
30g/1oz flour
225ml/8 fl oz chicken stock
225g/8oz green beans, sliced
120ml/4 fl oz Marsala
1 tbsp chopped parsley

Heat the butter or butter and oil in a frying pan, add the onions and sauté for 2 minutes. Remove from the pan. Sprinkle the veal cutlets with salt and pepper and dredge in the flour. Add to the frying pan and sauté on both sides for a few minutes. Lower the heat, add the stock, cover and cook for 20 minutes or until tender. Return the onions to the pan halfway through the cooking time. Meanwhile, cook the beans in boiling water for about 5-8 minutes. Drain and keep warm.

Remove the meat and onions and add the Marsala. Bring to the boil, stirring continuously. Arrange the cutlets on a serving dish, surrounded by the beans and onions. Cover with the sauce and sprinkle with chopped parsley.

Skewered Veal Birds

PREPARATION TIME: 25 minutes

COOKING TIME: 45 minutes

SERVES: 4 people

225g/8oz lean veal steak, cubed
225g/8oz fresh ham steak, cubed
120g/4oz pork liver
120g/4oz bacon, cubed
Fresh bay leaves
3 tbsps oil
7 tbsps dry white wine
120ml/4 fl oz chicken stock

This page: **Veal Cutlets with Vegetables.**
Facing page: **Skewered Veal Birds.**

POLENTA
490ml/17 fl oz water
2 tbsps salt
12oz cornmeal
120g/4oz Parmesan cheese, grated
Pepper

Put the veal, ham, liver and bacon cubes on long skewers, alternating various kinds of meat and occasionally putting a bay leaf between one piece and another. Heat the oil in a frying pan, add skewers and cook over high heat, turning occasionally. Add white wine and stock and cook for another 10 minutes, turning occasionally.

To prepare the polenta, bring the water and the salt to the boil in a

large pan and gradually stir in the cornmeal. Stir well to remove any lumps. Reduce the heat to low and partially cover. Continue cooking until the polenta is thick – about 30 minutes. Stir frequently and add more water if necessary to prevent sticking. Add the cheese and adjust the seasoning. Spread into a serving dish and lay the veal skewers on top.

Veal in Orange

PREPARATION TIME: 20 minutes
COOKING TIME: 1 hour 30 minutes
SERVES: 4 people

1kg/2.2lbs veal fillet
1 onion
570ml/1 pint chicken stock
Salt and pepper
2 oranges
4 small, young carrots
225g/8oz Italian rice
4 tbsps butter
3 tbsps flour
Pinch of powdered saffron
150ml/¼ pint double cream
Parsley to garnish

Dice the veal. Peel the onion and keep it whole. Put the veal, onion, stock and seasoning into a pan. Bring to the boil. Lower the heat and simmer for 40 minutes, until the meat is tender. Remove the onion. Cut away the peel from 1 orange, remove the white piths, then cut the orange peel into narrow strips. Soak in 150ml/¼ pint water for 30 minutes. Peel the carrots, cut into neat matchsticks, put with the orange rind and a little seasoning and simmer in a covered pan for 20 minutes. Remove the carrots and orange rind and cook the rice in the remaining salted water. Heat the butter in a pan, stir in the flour and cook for several minutes. Add the strained veal stock and bring to the boil. Cook until thickened. Add the orange rind, carrots, cooked rice and any liquid left, together with the pinch of saffron powder and the cream. Stir over a low heat until smooth. Add the cooked veal and

mix thoroughly. Arrange a border of rice with the remaining orange cut into slices on a serving dish. Spoon the veal mixture in the centre of the dish and sprinkle with parsley.

Veal with Tuna

PREPARATION TIME: 25 minutes
COOKING TIME: 1 hour 30 minutes
SERVES: 4-6 people

600g/1¼lbs boneless breast or shoulder
* of veal, in one piece*
Salt
1 stick celery, chopped
1 carrot
2 tbsps chopped parsley
1 tbsp chopped onion
1 small tin of flaked tuna
225ml/8 fl oz mayonnaise
2 tbsps capers
2 anchovy fillets in oil
225ml/8 fl oz dry white wine
10 pitted black olives

Trim the membranes from the veal. Put a little water and a few pinches of salt in a saucepan; add celery, carrot, parsley and onion. Heat and, when the water comes to the boil, add veal. Simmer for 1-1½ hours or until veal is tender. Drain and set aside to cool. Put the tuna through a food processor and blend it with the mayonnaise, half of the capers and anchovy fillets. Beat in the wine, which serves not only to smooth the sauce but to whiten it. Slice the veal and lay slices, overlapping, on a serving platter. Cover with tuna sauce. Sprinkle with the remaining capers and garnish with black olives. This sauce is also excellent on boiled beef.

Right: Veal in Orange (left) and Beef Scallops Tuscan Style (right).

Piquant Steak

PREPARATION TIME: 15 minutes

COOKING TIME: 15-20 minutes

SERVES: 4 people

680g/1¹/2lbs steak (sirloin or rump)
3 anchovy fillets, chopped
450g/1lb tomatoes, skinned, seeded and
    chopped
3 tbsps olive oil
2 tbsps capers
120ml/4 fl oz dry white wine
Salt and pepper

Cut the steak into strips about 7.5cm/
3 inches long and 1.25cm/¹/2 inch
thick. Mix together the anchovy
fillets and tomato pulp. Brown the
steak quickly in oil and remove to a
platter. Add tomato pulp mixture and
capers to pan juices. Heat until
bubbly. Stir in wine and pinch of
pepper and simmer until sauce is
thick. Season to taste with salt.
Return steak to the pan and cook to
desired degree, turning several times
in sauce and making sure that it is not
overcooked. Salt lightly and serve
immediately with pan juices spooned
over. Serve with freshly cooked pasta.

Beef Scallops Tuscan Style

PREPARATION TIME: 15 minutes

COOKING TIME: 15 minutes

SERVES: 4-6 people

680g/1¹/2lbs boneless beef round, sliced
    ¹/4-inch thick
Salt
Flour
1 egg, beaten
1¹/2 tbsps butter
2 tbsps olive oil
90ml/3 fl oz Marsala
1 tbsp tomato purée
4 anchovy fillets, chopped
1 tbsp capers, chopped
4 tomatoes, quartered

Pound the beef very thin, then
sprinkle with salt and flour on both
sides. Dip in the beaten egg. Heat the
butter and oil in a large frying pan.
Brown beef slices on both sides. Add
Marsala, raise heat slightly, and
simmer until wine evaporates. Place
beef slices on a platter and keep
warm. Into the same pan, add the
tomato purée mixed with ¹/2 cup water
and simmer for 5 minutes. Add the
anchovies and capers and simmer for
2 minutes more. Put the beef back in
the pan with the sauce and simmer
for 2-3 minutes over a low heat.
Garnish with tomatoes.

Piquant Pork Chops with Fennel

PREPARATION TIME: 30 minutes

COOKING TIME: 1 hour 10 minutes

OVEN TEMPERATURE:
180°C/350°F/Gas Mark 4

SERVES: 4 people

4 pork chops
1 tbsp oil
1 small onion, peeled and chopped
1 tbsp brown sugar
1 tbsp fennel seed
1 tbsp tomato purée
225ml/8 fl oz stock
225ml/8 fl oz red wine
2 tbsps lemon juice

Put the chops in a baking pan, or a
wide, shallow casserole and bake,
uncovered, at 180°C/350°F/Gas Mark
4 for about 20 minutes. Meanwhile,
heat the oil, add the onion and fry
until browned. Add the sugar, fennel
seed and tomato purée. Mix well then
add the stock and stir until boiling.
Add the wine and lemon juice and
check seasoning. Pour off any excess
fat from the chops and pour the sauce
over them. Cover and continue cooking
in the oven for about 40-45 minutes.

This page: Piquant Pork Chops with
Fennel. Facing page: Piquant Steak.

Chicken Cacciatore

PREPARATION TIME: 15 minutes

COOKING TIME: 30 minutes

SERVES: 4 people

3 tbsps olive oil
460g/1lb chicken breast, cut into bite-
   sized pieces
1 tsp basil
1 tsp oregano
1 bay leaf
1 onion, peeled and sliced
2 cloves garlic, crushed
1 green pepper, cored, seeds removed,
   and sliced
120g/4oz mushrooms, sliced
460g/16oz tin plum tomatoes
2 tsps tomato purée
150ml/5 fl oz dry white wine
Salt and pepper

GARNISH
Parsley

Heat a frying pan and add 1 tbsp oil.
When hot, add the chicken and stir-
fry until it is opaque – about 8
minutes. Add more oil if necessary.
Remove with a slotted spoon and set
aside. Heat the remaining oil, add
basil, oregano and bay leaf and fry for
1 minute. Add the onion and garlic,
and stir-fry until the onion is soft but
not coloured. Add the green pepper
and mushrooms and fry for a further 3
minutes. Add undrained tomatoes,
tomato purée, wine and salt and pepper
to taste. Cook, uncovered, for 10
minutes. Return the chicken to the
pan and stir until heated through.
Garnish with parsley and serve with
spaghetti.

Lemon Chicken

PREPARATION TIME: 5 minutes

COOKING TIME: 40 minutes

SERVES: 4 people

900g/2lbs chicken pieces
75ml/2½ fl oz oil

LEMON SAUCE
2 tsps cornflour
75ml/2½ fl oz water
Juice of 1 lemon
2 tbsps sweet sherry
Pinch of sugar if required

GARNISH
Lemon slices

Heat a frying pan and add the oil. When
hot, add the chicken pieces and stir-fry
in the oil until well browned. Reduce
heat, cover and simmer for 30 minutes,
or until chicken is cooked. Remove
with a slotted spoon and drain on
kitchen paper. Place the chicken pieces
in a serving dish and keep warm. Meanwhile, carefully drain the oil from the
pan. Slake cornflour with 2 tbsps of the
water. Put the lemon juice and
remaining water in the pan and bring to
the boil. Add the cornflour and stir
until boiling. Simmer for 2 minutes
until thickened. Add the sherry and
sugar and simmer for a further 2 minutes.
Pour sauce over the chicken pieces and
garnish with lemon slices. Serve with
boiled rice.

Turkey Cutlets with Lemon Sauce

PREPARATION TIME: 30 minutes

COOKING TIME: 20 minutes

SERVES: 6 people

6 turkey cutlets
Salt and pepper
2 tbsps flour
2 thick-cut slices of ham
2 tbsps butter
300ml/½ pint chicken stock
Juice of 1 lemon
2 tbsps chopped parsley

GARNISH
Lemon slices
Sprigs of parsley

Season flour and coat the turkey cutlets.
Cut the ham into strips. Melt the butter
in a frying pan and cook the ham for 5
minutes. Add the turkey pieces and fry
for 3-5 minutes on each side. Remove
the turkey and keep warm. Add any
remaining seasoned flour to the pan
and stir well with a wooden spoon,
scraping the sediment from the bottom
of the pan. Gradually add the stock and
bring to the boil; simmer for 5 minutes.
Remove from the heat and stir in the
lemon juice and chopped parsley. Taste
and adjust seasoning. Pour the sauce
over the turkey cutlets and garnish with
lemon slices and sprigs of parsley.

Chicken Cacciatore (left) and Lemon
Chicken (below).

Piquant Liver

PREPARATION TIME: 15 minutes

COOKING TIME: 20 minutes

SERVES: 4 people

1 tbsp flour
Salt and pepper
460g/1lb liver, cut into thin strips
60g/2oz butter or margarine
1 onion, finely sliced
2 tbsps wine vinegar
90ml/3 fl oz white wine
1 tbsp chopped parsley

GARNISH
Chopped parsley

Combine the flour with a good pinch of salt and freshly ground black pepper. Toss in the liver and coat well. Heat half the butter in a frying pan over a gentle heat. Add the onion and fry gently until transparent. Add the vinegar and cook over a high heat until the vinegar has evaporated. Add the remaining butter and when hot add the liver. Fry quickly for about 3 minutes. Add the wine, parsley and salt and pepper to taste. Bring to the boil and simmer for 5 minutes. Sprinkle with chopped parsley and serve with rice.

Sicilian Roast Lamb

PREPARATION TIME: 20 minutes

COOKING TIME: 20 minutes per 460g/1lb plus 20 minutes

OVEN TEMPERATURE: 220°C/425°F/Gas Mark 7

SERVES: 6-8 people

1 leg of lamb
4 tbsps butter
Salt and pepper
Rosemary
1 clove garlic
120g/4oz dry breadcrumbs
900g/2lbs new potatoes

Stick rosemary leaves into the fat of the meat. Insert a clove of garlic near the bone. Spread butter over the

lamb and season well. Press breadcrumbs over the surface of the lamb. Place the joint on a rack in a roasting pan and roast in the centre of a preheated oven. Place sliced potatoes under the meat after it has been cooking for 30 minutes. Baste the joint from time to time.

Liver with Oranges

PREPARATION TIME: 20 minutes

COOKING TIME: 15-20 minutes

SERVES: 4 people

340g/12oz liver, sliced
2 tbsps flour
Salt and pepper
2 tbsps butter
1 tbsp olive oil
1 onion, sliced
1 clove garlic, crushed
150ml/5 fl oz brown stock

Juice and grated rind of 1 orange
2 oranges, peeled and sliced, for garnish

Dredge the liver slices with flour and season with salt and pepper. Heat the oil in a frying pan and drop in the butter. When the fat is hot, add the liver and cook until browned on both sides – about 5 minutes. Cook in two batches if necessary. Remove the liver and add the onion to the pan. Cook until beginning to brown and add the garlic. Add any remaining flour and pour on the stock and orange juice. Add the orange rind and stir to mix well, scraping any sediment from the bottom of the pan. Add the liver, cover the pan and simmer for 10-15 minutes, or until the liver is tender. Serve with rice and pasta and garnish with orange slices.

This page: Piquant Liver. Facing page: Liver with Oranges.

Lamb Chops with Mushrooms

PREPARATION TIME: 40 minutes

COOKING TIME: 45 minutes

SERVES: 4 people

4 tbsps olive oil
4 loin chops
1 onion, sliced
2 tbsps flour
225ml/8 fl oz dry white wine
225ml/8 fl oz chicken stock
1 tbsp Marsala
Salt and pepper
120g/4oz button mushrooms
2 tomatoes, skinned and quartered
Chopped parsley

Heat the oil and brown the chops on both sides. Drain and leave on one side. Add the onion to the pan and cook, with the flour, until soft. Allow to cool slightly then pour on the wine, stock and Marsala. Return the chops to the pan, season well, bring to the boil, reduce the heat and simmer, covered, for about 30 minutes. Add the mushrooms and tomatoes. Adjust seasoning and simmer for a further 15 minutes. Place the chops on a serving dish, spoon over the sauce and garnish with chopped parsley.

ITALIAN COOKING

DESSERTS, CAKES & BISCUITS

Chestnut Parfait

PREPARATION TIME:
40 minutes plus freezing

SERVES: 4 people

4 egg yolks
4 tbsps sugar
175ml/6 fl oz milk, warmed and
flavoured with a vanilla pod
225g/8oz unsweetened chestnut purée
2 tbsps Marsala
2 egg whites
6 tbsps sugar
570ml/1 pint double cream

Beat the egg yolks with the sugar and
add the warmed milk flavoured with
the vanilla pod and cook until
thickened, stirring gently. The
mixture should coat the spoon.
Transfer to a mixing bowl. Add the
chestnut purée and Marsala while the
mixture is still lukewarm. Chill well.
Whip the egg whites with the sugar
until very stiff. Beat the cream until it
peaks. Fold the egg white into the
chestnut cream and carefully fold in
the whipped cream. Pour into a bowl
and freeze for 4 hours. Remove from
the freezer ½ hour before serving.
Spoon into individual glass dishes to
serve.

Facing page: Lamb Chops with
Mushrooms. **This page:** Chestnut
Parfait.

Ricotta Pancakes with Honey and Raisin Sauce

PREPARATION TIME: 10 minutes

COOKING TIME: 2-3 minutes

SERVES: 4 people

SAUCE
4 tbsps clear honey
Juice of ½ lemon
1 tbsp raisins
1 tbsp pine kernels

FILLING
225g/8oz ricotta cheese
Grated rind of ½ lemon
2 tbsps raisins
1 tbps chopped pine kernels

8 small, hot pancakes

TO DECORATE
Twists of lemon

To make the sauce, put all the ingredients into a small pan and warm through gently. For the filling, beat the cheese and the lemon rind until soft; mix in the raisins and pine kernels. Divide the filling among the hot pancakes and either roll them up or fold them into triangles. Arrange the pancakes on warm plates, spoon the sauce over the top and decorate with twists of lemon. Serve immediately.

Almond-stuffed Figs

PREPARATION TIME: 25 minutes

SERVES: 4 people

4 large ripe figs
30g/4 tbsps ground almonds
2 tbsps orange juice
2 tbsps finely chopped dried apricots

SAUCE
60ml/4 tbsps cream
Finely grated rind of ½ orange

GARNISH
Wedges of ripe fig
Wedges of lime
Ground cinnamon

Make a cross cut in each fig without cutting right down and through the base. Ease the four sections of each fig out, rather like a flower head. Mix the ground almonds with the orange juice and chopped dried apricots; press into the centre of each fig. For the sauce: mix the cream with the orange rind and thin down with a little water. Spoon a pool of orange-flavoured cream onto each of 4 small plates; place a stuffed fig in the centre of each one. Decorate with wedges of fig and lime and a sprinkling of ground cinnamon.

Lime and Chocolate Gâteau

PREPARATION TIME: 35 minutes

COOKING TIME: 20 minutes

OVEN TEMPERATURE:
190°C/375°C/Gas Mark 5

125g/4oz sugar
3 eggs
75g/3oz flour
Grated rind of 1 lime
Flesh of 1 lime, seeded
2 tbsps melted butter

DECORATION
300ml/½ pint double cream
1 fresh lime
Grated chocolate (optional)

Beat the sugar and eggs together in a basin, over a saucepan of hot water, until the mixture is thick. Fold the flour into the beaten mixture. Mix in the lime flesh and grated rind. Grease and flour a 20cm/ 8-inch cake tin and fill with the mixture. Bake in the oven for 20 minutes. Cool on a wire rack.

TO DECORATE
Whip the cream and spread over the gâteau, reserving a little for decorating. Fill a piping bag with the remaining cream and, using a star nozzle, shape rosettes to decorate the gâteau. Sprinkle the sides with chocolate, if wished, and decorate with slices of lime.

Ricotta Pancakes with Honey and Raisin Sauce (right) and Almond-stuffed Figs (below).

Profiteroles

PREPARATION TIME:
1 hour 30 minutes

COOKING TIME: 30 minutes

OVEN TEMPERATURE:
160°c/325°F/Gas Mark 3

MAKES: 18 profiteroles

CHOUX PASTRY
120g/4oz plain flour, sieved
Pinch of salt
75g/2½oz butter
225g/8 fl oz water
3 eggs

FILLING
600ml/1 pint double cream
2 tbsps sieved icing sugar
2 tbsps Liquore alla Mandarina

CARAMEL
225g/8oz caster sugar

120ml/4 fl oz water

Sift the flour and salt together. Melt the butter in a heavy saucepan with the water and bring to the boil. Remove from the heat. Add the flour and salt mixture to the pan, all in one go, as soon as the liquid has boiled. Beat vigorously with a wooden spoon until the mixture leaves the sides of the pan and forms a ball. Beat in the eggs, one at a time, beating well after each addition until the paste is smooth and silky. Fit a piping bag with a 2cm/¾-inch plain nozzle and fill with the paste. Pipe about 18 balls onto two greased baking sheets, leaving 5cm/2-inch gaps in between. Bake for 25-30 minutes until well risen, firm and golden brown. Pierce a hole in the base of each puff to allow the steam to escape and return to the oven

for two minutes. Cool on a wire rack.

FILLING
Whip the cream, fold in the sugar and the liqueur. Fill a piping bag fitted with a plain nozzle with the cream and fill each of the profiteroles.

CARAMEL
Dissolve the sugar gently in a saucepan with the water, then boil it, without stirring, until it turns brown and caramelizes. Cool until the caramel begins to thicken but not set and pour quickly, but gently, over the profiteroles. Leave to set and chill for ½ hour before serving.

This page: **Profiteroles (left) and Lime and Chocolate Gâteau (right). Facing page: Vanilla Cream Melba (top) and Chocolate Cream Helène (bottom).**

Vanilla Cream Melba

PREPARATION TIME: 15 minutes

COOKING TIME: 10 minutes

SERVES: 4 people

90g/3oz soup pasta
420ml/³/4 pint milk
45g/1¹/2oz brown sugar
Few drops vanilla essence
140ml/¹/4 pint double cream, lightly
    whipped
1 x 400g/14oz tin peach halves
1 tsp cinnamon

MELBA SAUCE
225g/8oz raspberries
30g/1oz icing sugar

Cook the pasta in the milk and sugar until soft. Stir regularly, being careful not to allow it to boil over. Draw off the heat and stir in the vanilla essence. Pour the pasta into a bowl to cool. When cool, fold in the cream. Chill. Meanwhile, make the Melba sauce. Push the raspberries through a fine nylon sieve. Mix in the icing sugar to the required thickness and taste. Serve the pasta with the peach halves and Melba sauce. Dust with a little cinnamon to serve.

Chocolate Cream Helène

PREPARATION TIME: 15 minutes

COOKING TIME: 10 minutes

SERVES: 4 people

90g/3oz soup pasta
450ml/15 fl oz milk
2¹/2 tbsps sugar
1 tsp cocoa
1 tbsp hot water
150ml/5 fl oz cream, lightly whipped
1 large tin pear halves

GARNISH
Grated chocolate

Cook the pasta in the milk and sugar until soft. Stir regularly, being careful not to allow it to boil over. Meanwhile, dissolve the cocoa in hot water and stir into the pasta. Pour the pasta into a bowl to cool. When cool, fold in the lightly-whipped cream. Chill. Serve with pear halves and a sprinkling of grated chocolate.

Black Cherry Ravioli with Soured Cream Sauce

PREPARATION TIME: 30 minutes

COOKING TIME: 15 minutes

SERVES: 4 people

DOUGH
275g/10oz strong plain flour
1 tbsp sugar
3 eggs, lightly beaten

Large tin dark, sweet cherries, stoned
1 tbsp sugar
1 tsp cornflour
120ml/4 fl oz soured cream
120ml/4 fl oz double cream

Strain the cherries and reserve the juice. Make the dough by sifting the flour and sugar into a bowl. Make a well in the centre and add the lightly-beaten eggs. Work the flour and eggs together with a spoon and then by hand until a smooth dough is formed. Knead gently. Lightly flour a board, and roll the dough out thinly into a rectangle. Cut the dough in half. Put the well-drained cherries about 4cm/1¹/2 inches apart on the dough. Place the other half on top and cut with a small glass or pastry cutter. Seal well around the edges with the back of a fork. Boil plenty of water in a large saucepan and drop in cherry pasta. Cook for about 10 minutes, or until they rise to the surface. Remove with a slotted spoon and keep warm. Keep 2 tbsps cherry juice aside. Mix 1 tbsp cherry juice with the cornflour; mix remaining juice with sugar and set over heat. Add the cornflour mixture and heat until it thickens. Meanwhile, mix soured cream and double cream together and marble 1 tbsp of the cherry juice through it. Pour hot, thickened cherry juice over the cherry ravioli. Serve with the hot cream sauce.

Right: Black Cherry Ravioli with Soured Cream Sauce.

Honey Vermicelli

PREPARATION TIME: 1 hour

COOKING TIME: 15 minutes

SERVES: 4 people

225g/8oz vermicelli
60g/2oz butter
2 tsps sesame seeds
3 tbsps clear honey
1/4 tsp grated cinnamon

SAUCE
120ml/4 fl oz double cream
120ml/4 fl oz soured cream

Cook the vermicelli in boiling salted water for 5 minutes or until tender, stirring regularly with a fork to separate the noodles. Drain and spread out to dry on a wire rack covered with absorbent paper or a tea towel. Leave for about 1 hour. Make the sauce by mixing the soured cream and double cream together. Melt the butter in a frying pan. Add the sesame seeds, and fry until lightly golden. Stir in the honey, cinnamon and vermicelli, and heat through. Serve hot, topped with the cream sauce.

Cream Cheese Margherita

PREPARATION TIME: 1 hour

COOKING TIME: 10 minutes

SERVES: 4 people

60g/2oz sultanas
Juice and grated rind of 1/2 lemon
120g/4oz soup pasta
1 x 225g/8oz pack cream cheese
60g/2oz caster sugar
140ml/1/4 pint single cream
1/2 tsp ground cinnamon

DECORATION
1 tbsp flaked almonds
Julienned lemon zest

Soak the sultanas in the lemon juice for about 1 hour. Meanwhile, cook the pasta in plenty of boiling, lightly salted water until tender, stirring occasionally. Work the cream cheese, sugar and cream together until smooth. Beat in the grated lemon rind and cinnamon. Fold in the pasta and sultanas. To serve, chill and decorate with the flaked almonds and lemon zest.

Chocolate Apricot Horns

PREPARATION TIME: 15 minutes

COOKING TIME: 15-20 minutes

OVEN TEMPERATURE:
220°C/425°F/Gas Mark 7

MAKES: 10

225g/8oz puff pastry
Beaten egg to glaze
120g/4oz plain chocolate
15g/1/2oz butter
2 tbsps brandy
175ml/6 fl oz apricot purée
175ml/6 fl oz double cream

TO DECORATE
Chocolate curls

Roll the pastry out into a rectangle about 25x33cm/10x3 inches and trim the edges. Cut into strips 2.5cm/1-inch wide. Dampen one long edge of each strip with water and wind round a metal cornet mould (start at the point and overlap the dampened edge as you go). Put the horns on a lightly dampened baking sheet and chill for 15 minutes. Brush the horns with beaten egg and bake in an oven pre-heated to 220°C/425°F/Gas Mark 7 for 15-20 minutes, or until golden brown. Leave for 5 minutes before carefully removing the moulds; cool the pastry horns on a wire rack. Melt the chocolate with the butter on a plate over a pan of hot water; dip each of the horns into the chocolate. Mix the brandy with the apricot purée and spoon a little into each of the horns. Fit a star nozzle to a piping bag and fill with the whipped cream. Pipe the cream into the horns. Decorate with chocolate curls.

Honey Vermicelli (above right) and Cream Cheese Margherita (right).

Profiteroles Vine

PREPARATION TIME:
30 minutes, plus cooling

COOKING TIME: 40-45 minutes

OVEN TEMPERATURE: 200°C/
400°F/Gas Mark 6

SERVES: 4-6 people

PASTRY
150ml/5 fl oz water
50g/2oz butter
75g/2¹/₂oz flour, sieved
2 eggs, beaten

FILLING
150ml/5 fl oz double cream, whipped
1 tbsp sugar
1 tbsp cocoa
175g/6oz plain chocolate, melted

SAUCE
3 tbsps strong black coffee
225g/8oz plain chocolate, chopped or grated
150ml/5 fl oz double cream
3 tbsps apricot jam

To make the pastry, heat the water and butter in a small saucepan until the butter melts. Bring to the boil, remove the pan from the heat and beat in the flour. Beat with a wooden spoon until the mixture leaves the sides of the pan clean. Cool the mixture slightly and gradually beat in the eggs, beating between each addition (the mixture should be smooth and glossy). Fill a piping bag fitted with a large plain nozzle with the pastry. Pipe 20 even-sized balls onto two dampened baking sheets. Bake in a preheated oven for 20-25 minutes until well risen. Split each of the balls and let the steam escape; return to the oven for a further 2 minutes. To make the filling, whip the cream with the sugar. When peaks form, fold in the cocoa. Fill a large piping bag, fitted with a plain nozzle, with the cream and fill the choux buns. To decorate and serve, coat a large, clean leaf with melted chocolate; pipe a few curls and a stem onto a sheet of greaseproof paper. Leave them to set; gently peel off the

paper and the leaf. Arrange the profiteroles to look like a bunch of grapes on a large serving tray or dish; add the chocolate leaf, stems and curls. To make the sauce, put all the ingredients into a small, heavy-based pan. Stir continuously over a low heat until smooth. Finally, pour the chocolate over the profiteroles.

Avocado Cheesecake

PREPARATION TIME:
30 minutes, plus chilling

CHEESECAKE BASE
225g/8oz chocolate digestive biscuits
90g/3oz butter, melted

FILLING
2 ripe avocado pears
Juice of ¹/₂ a lemon
Grated rind of 1 lemon

This page: Avocado Cheesecake. Facing page: Profiteroles Vine (top) and Chocolate Apricot Horns (bottom).

120g/4oz cream cheese
75g/3oz caster sugar
2 tsps gelatine powder
2 egg whites
150ml/5 fl oz double cream, whipped

DECORATION
150ml/5 fl oz double cream, whipped

Crush the biscuits into fine crumbs and stir in the melted butter. Use the mixture to line the base and sides of a 19cm/7¹/₂-inch springform tin. Chill well.

FOR THE FILLING
Peel and stone the avocados and save a few slices for decoration. Put the remainder into a bowl and mash well.

Mix in the lemon juice and grated rind, cream cheese and sugar. Beat until smooth. Dissolve the gelatine in 2 tbsps of hot water and stir into the mixture. Beat the egg whites in a clean, dry bowl and fold into the mixture with the whipped cream. Pour into the prepared biscuit base and chill thoroughly until set.

TO DECORATE

Carefully remove the cheesecake from the tin. Fill a pastry bag, fitted with a star tube, with the cream reserved for decoration. Decorate a border of cream round the edge of the cake. Decorate with avocado slices.

NB: sprinkle the avocado with lemon juice to prevent it from discolouring.

Chocolate Chip Ice Cream

PREPARATION TIME:
30 minutes, plus freezing time
COOKING TIME: 6-8 minutes
SERVES: 4 people

120g/4oz plain chocolate, chopped or grated
280ml/¹/² pint milk
3 egg yolks
90g/3oz sugar
280ml/¹/² pint double cream, lightly whipped
75g/2¹/² oz finely chopped chocolate

Stir the chopped or grated chocolate into the milk in a small, heavy-based saucepan; stir over a gentle heat until the chocolate has melted. Put the egg yolks into a bowl with the sugar and beat until thick and creamy. Add the chocolate milk and beat. Return the chocolate mixture to the saucepan and stir continuously over a moderate heat until the mixture is thick and will coat the back of a spoon. Strain the chocolate custard into a bowl and cool in the refrigerator. When quite cold, fold in the whipped cream. Pour into ice trays and freeze until the mixture begins to set around the edges. Pour into a bowl and beat. Stir

in the chopped chocolate. Return the ice cream to the ice trays and freeze for 30 minutes, or until beginning to set. Repeat the beating and freezing method every 30 minutes until the ice cream is thick. Turn into a cold 1.1 litre/2-pint container and freeze until firm.

Chocolate Ice Box Cake

PREPARATION TIME:
1 hour, plus freezing
COOKING TIME: 25-30 minutes
OVEN TEMPERATURE:
190°C/375°F/Gas Mark 5
SERVES: 8 people

Melted butter for greasing
7 eggs, separated
75g/3oz vanilla sugar
5 tbsps flour
Pinch of salt
Sugar

FILLING

340g/12oz plain chocolate, chopped or grated
2 tbsps strong black coffee
60ml/2 fl oz maraschino liqueur
2 egg yolks
5 egg whites, stiffly beaten
120ml/4 fl oz double cream, lightly whipped

ICING

150ml/5 fl oz double cream
150g/5oz plain chocolate, chopped or grated

Grease and line two 23x30cm/9x12-inch Swiss roll tins with greaseproof paper. Brush the paper with melted butter and dust with flour. Beat the egg yolks and vanilla sugar together until thick and light; fold in the flour and salt. Beat the egg whites until stiff but not dry. Gently fold the beaten egg whites into the mixture. Divide the mixture between the two tins. Bake in a preheated oven for 15-20 minutes, or until golden. When the cakes are baked, spread two towels on a work surface and cover each one with a sheet of greaseproof

paper. Sprinkle with sugar and turn the cakes out onto the sugared paper. Peel off the lining paper and leave the sponges to cool. Line the bottom of a 20cm/8-inch springform cake tin with greased greaseproof paper. Cut a circle of cake from each rectangular sponge to fit the pan. Put one on top of the paper lining. Reserve the other. Cut three strips of cake, 5cm/2 inches wide, to line the sides of the tin. Place in position. To make the filling, put the chocolate, coffee and maraschino into a saucepan and stir over a low heat until the chocolate has melted. Leave to cool. Beat in the egg yolks and then gently fold in the beaten egg whites, taking care not to over-mix. Finally, fold in the whipped double cream. Pour the mixture into the cake-lined tin and put the remaining cake circle on top as a lid. Cover the top of the pan with a plate 20cm/8 inches in diameter, weighted down lightly. Put the cake tin into the freezer for 2-3 hours, or chill in the refrigerator for at least 5 hours. To make the icing, pour the cream into a pan and bring to the boil. Stir in the chocolate until it melts and the mixture thickens. Carefully take the set cake out of its pan and pour icing over it. Open freeze, or refrigerate, until the frosting has set.

Facing page: Chocolate Chip Ice Cream (top) and Chocolate Ice Box Cake (bottom).

Artichoke

PREPARATION TIME: 1 hour 30 minutes, plus setting overnight

MAKES:
1 artichoke, serving 8-10 people

450g/1lb plain chocolate, chopped or
    grated
2 tbsps oil
Few drops of almond essence
1 globe artichoke

TO MAKE THE ARTICHOKE
2 tbsps sugar
2 tbsps butter
2 tbsps water
60g/2oz icing sugar, sieved
2 tbsps cocoa
A piece of cake the size of the artichoke

Melt the chocolate with the oil, stirring occasionally until melted. Cool the mixture slightly and stir in the almond essence. Take the leaves off the artichoke; dip the front of each leaf into the melted chocolate and lay them on greaseproof paper. Leave overnight to set before peeling off the artichoke leaves. To make the icing, dissolve the sugar in the butter and water over a low heat; remove from the heat and stir in the icing sugar and the cocoa. Cut the cake into a pyramid shape and cover it with some of the cooled icing. Stick the chocolate artichoke leaves around the cake in the same order as the real artichoke was assembled. You will need to use some of the icing to help them to stick.

This page: Artichoke. Facing page: Apricot Ice Roll.

Truffles

PREPARATION TIME: 15 minutes

MAKES: about 10

120g/4oz plain chocolate, chopped or grated
1 tbsp Marsala
30g/1oz unsalted butter
1 egg yolk
120g/4oz ground almonds
120g/4oz cake crumbs
60g/2oz chocolate vermicelli

Melt the chocolate with the Marsala in a small bowl over a saucepan of hot water. Beat in the butter and egg yolk and remove the mixture from the heat. Stir in the ground almonds and cake crumbs to make a smooth paste. Divide into balls and roll them in the vermicelli until evenly coated.

Honey Ice Cream

PREPARATION TIME:
15 minutes, plus freezing

460g/1lb raspberries
150ml/5 fl oz clear honey
120ml/4 fl oz water
4 tbsps granulated sugar
150ml/5 fl oz double cream
150ml/5 fl oz single cream
3 egg whites
2 tbsps lemon juice

Cook the raspberries in a saucepan with the honey and water. Add the sugar and cook for 5 minutes until dissolved. Leave to cool. Rub the mixture through a sieve and chill. Beat the double cream until thick and stir in the single cream. Fold the creams into the fruit mixture. Freeze until almost solid. Whisk egg whites with the lemon juice until foaming. Whisk in the sugar a table-spoon at a time until a glossy meringue is formed. Beat the frozen mixture and fold in the meringue. Re-freeze until solid.

Apricot Ice Roll

PREPARATION TIME:
35 minutes, plus freezing

COOKING TIME: 12 minutes

OVEN TEMPERATURE:
220°C/425°F/Gas Mark 7

CAKE MIXTURE
2 eggs
60g/2oz sugar
60g/2oz flour

FILLING AND DECORATING
4 tbsps apricot jam
570ml/1 pint soft-scoop vanilla ice cream
Cream to decorate
Apricots, halved

Beat the eggs and sugar until light and fluffy. Carefully fold in the flour. Turn into a greased and floured Swiss roll tin and bake. Turn out onto a clean cloth and leave to cool. Spread the sponge with apricot jam and softened ice cream. Roll up using a clean cloth. Place in the freezer until ice cream is hardened. Decorate with cream and sliced apricots.

Zabaglione

PREPARATION TIME: 5 minutes

COOKING TIME: 10 minutes

4 egg yolks
4 tbsps sugar
4 tbsps Marsala wine

Put the ingredients into a heatproof bowl. Beat with a wire whisk until light and frothy. Stand the bowl in a pan of water over a low heat and continue to beat. The mixture will froth and is ready to serve. Pour into heatproof glasses and serve with sponge fingers.

This page: **Truffles.** Facing page:
Apricot Ice (top), **Minted Lime Ice**
(centre left), **Honey Ice Cream** (centre
right) and **Lemon Ice Cream Torte**
(bottom).

Apricot Ice

PREPARATION TIME:
15 minutes, plus freezing

75g/3oz caster sugar
420ml/15 fl oz water
1 small tin apricots, puréed
Juice of 3 lemons
3 tbsps Curaçao
3 egg whites, beaten

Dissolve the sugar in the water over a low heat and boil for 10 minutes. Leave to cool. Blend apricots with lemon juice and Curaçao. Add the apricot syrup. Pour into a container and freeze until just frozen. Turn into a bowl. Fold in the beaten egg whites. Freeze.

Lemon Ice Cream Torte

PREPARATION TIME:
20 minutes, plus freezing
COOKING TIME: 15 minutes
OVEN TEMPERATURE:
220°C/425°F/Gas Mark 7

TORTE
3 large eggs
75g/3oz sugar
75g/3oz plain flour, sieved
1 tsp baking powder

FILLING
Grated rind and juice of 1 lemon
6 scoops soft vanilla ice cream

TO DECORATE
Icing sugar
Sugared lemon peel

To make the torte, beat the eggs and sugar until light and fluffy. Sift in the flour and baking powder and mix in carefully. Bake in a large 13cm/5-inch baking tin. Turn out to cool. When cool, slice the cake into 3 layers, horizontally. Mix together the lemon rind and juice and the vanilla ice cream. Spread the mixture on the layers, sandwich together and freeze. Dust with icing sugar and add lemon peel to decorate.

Minted Lime Ice

PREPARATION TIME:
15 minutes, plus freezing

175g/6oz caster sugar
420ml/15 fl oz water
Grated rind and juice of 6 limes
4 tbsps fresh mint, finely chopped
150ml/5 fl oz double cream
3 tbsps single cream

Place the sugar and water in a saucepan. Stir gently over a low heat. When the sugar has dissolved bring the mixture to the boil. Remove from the heat. Stir in the grated rind, lime juice and the mint. Let the mixture cool and pour into ice trays. Cover with foil and freeze. When the mixture is frozen, crush it. Lightly whip the creams together. Stir the lime ice into the cream and refreeze. To serve, thaw slightly and spoon into small glasses.

Marsala Ice Cream Torte

PREPARATION TIME:
30 minutes, plus freezing time
COOKING TIME: 1 hour
OVEN TEMPERATURE:
150°C/300°F/Gas Mark 2
SERVES: 6-8 people

Oil for greasing
3 egg whites
225g/8oz sugar
1 tbsp instant coffee
2 tbsps boiling water
420ml/¾ pint cream
2 tbsps Marsala
280ml/½ pint chocolate ice cream, softened

Lightly oil a baking sheet and line the base of an 8cm/7-inch round, loose-bottomed cake tin with greaseproof paper. Whisk the egg whites, gradually add the sugar and continue to whisk until stiff. Add the remaining sugar and whisk until the mixture peaks. Fill a piping bag fitted with a star nozzle with the meringue mixture. Pipe small rosettes onto the baking sheet, keeping them well apart. Bake in a preheated oven for 1 hour; leave in the oven for a further 20 minutes with the oven turned off. Remove the meringues from the oven and allow them to cool. Mix the coffee with the water in a small bowl. Whip the cream until thick; fold in all but 4 of the meringues. Add the coffee and the Marsala, taking care not to crush the meringues. Fold in the ice cream. Use the mixture to fill the prepared cake tin. Cover and freeze until firm. Put the reserved meringues in the centre of the torte and decorate the top with piped whipped cream and grated chocolate or cocoa if wished. Remove from the freezer to the refrigerator 10-15 minutes before serving.

Mocha Ice Cream

PREPARATION TIME:
25 minutes, plus freezing
SERVES: 6 people

2 tbsps instant coffee granules
4 tbsps butter
120g/4oz soft brown sugar
4 tbsps cocoa
5 tbsps water
420ml/¾ pint evaporated milk, chilled

Put the coffee, butter, sugar, cocoa and water into a saucepan and heat gently. Stir the mixture until melted and bring to the boil. Cool. Beat the chilled evaporated milk in a bowl until it is thick and frothy. Mix it into the cooled mixture, beating until it is well blended. Pour the mixture into a freezer container and freeze, uncovered, until slushy. Beat the ice cream well and refreeze until firm.

Facing page: Mocha Ice Cream (top) and Marsala Ice Cream Torte (bottom).

Pear, Raisin and Marsala Ice

PREPARATION TIME: 10 minutes, plus soaking and freezing time

1 small tin of pears, puréed
50g/2oz caster sugar
100g/4oz raisins
1 egg white, stiffly beaten

Put the pear purée in a pan with the sugar and heat gently until the sugar has dissolved. Boil quickly for 5 minutes and remove from the heat. Cool. Soak raisins in Marsala and add enough pear syrup to cover the mixture. Soak for 4 hours, then mix the raisins and Marsala with the pear purée in a shallow container and freeze. Mash with a fork and fold in the beaten egg whites. Return to the freezer. Serve frozen in glasses.

Red Wine Granita

PREPARATION TIME:
15 minutes, plus freezing

90g/3oz sugar
Juice of ¹/₂ lime and ¹/₂ orange
1 tbsp water
Small bunch lemon balm leaves
¹/₂ bottle Lambrusco
Lemon rind

Boil half the sugar with the lime juice, orange juice, water and the balm leaves. Cool, strain and add to the wine. Freeze in a shallow container. To serve: scrape the granita with a spoon to produce ice shavings and serve shavings in glasses, decorated with lemon rind.

This page: Zuppa Inglese. Facing page: **Red Wine Granita** (top), **Pear, Raisin and Marsala Ice** (centre), and **Asti Spumante Ice** (bottom).

Zuppa Inglese

PREPARATION TIME: 45 minutes

SERVES: 8 people

12 sponge fingers or 1 sponge cake
60g/2oz ratafia biscuits
60g/2oz flaked almonds
60ml/2 fl oz Amaretto

CUSTARD
2 tbsps cornflour
2 tbsps sugar
300ml/½ pint milk
1 egg, lightly beaten
Pinch cinnamon
300ml/½ pint whipped cream (not too
   stiff)
Few glacé cherries

Crumble the ratafias. Slice the sponge-
fingers in half, or the cake into strips,
and line the bottom of a glass serving
bowl. Sprinkle with some ratafias and
flaked almonds and the Amaretto.
Put the cornflour and sugar in a small
mixing bowl, mix with 2 tbsps of the
milk and bring the rest of the milk to
the boil. Pour it over the cornflour
mixture, stirring all the time. Return
the pan to the heat, bring the custard
back to the boil and simmer for one
minute. Remove from the heat and
beat in the lightly beaten egg. Cool
and, when lukewarm, pour over the
cake. When quite cold, top with
whipped cream and sprinkle on the
remainder of the ratafias, almonds and
a few pieces of chopped glacé cherry.

Asti Spumante Ice

PREPARATION TIME:
5 minutes, plus freezing time

SERVES: 6 people

⅔ bottle Asti Spumante
Fresh blackcurrants and raspberries
Sugar to dust

Freeze the Asti Spumante in a
shallow container. When frozen,
scrape off into glasses. Decorate with
blackcurrants and raspberries and dust
with sugar.

Zuppa alla Romana

PREPARATION TIME: 20 minutes

SERVES: 6 people

1 large sponge cake, sliced
6 tbsps apricot jam
120ml/4 fl oz Curaçao
450ml/¾ pint cold, thick custard
300ml/½ pint double cream
3 tsps icing sugar
Toasted flaked almonds
Crystallised orange peel cut into strips

Line the bottom of a glass dish with half
the cake. Sprinkle half the Curaçao
over the cake. Spread the jam on top of
the cake and cover with the remaining
slices. Pour over the remaining Curaçao.
Spoon the custard over the cake. Whip
the cream and gradually add icing sugar
until it peaks. Spoon the cream over
the custard and decorate with lightly
toasted flaked almond and strips of
candied orange peel.

Pears in Wine

PREPARATION TIME:
15 minutes, plus chilling

COOKING TIME: 30 minutes

SERVES: 6 people

250g/9oz sugar
120ml/4 fl oz water
6 large pears, peeled
1 cinnamon stick
1 piece lemon peel
225ml/8 fl oz sweet red wine

Gently heat the sugar and water until
the sugar has dissolved. Add the pears,
cinnamon and lemon peel and cover.
Simmer for 15 minutes. Stir in the wine
and continue to simmer, uncovered, for
another 15 minutes. Remove the pears
from the saucepan and arrange in a
serving dish. Bring the wine syrup back
to the boil until thick. Pour over the
pears and allow to cool. Serve chilled.

Chocolate Ice Cream

PREPARATION TIME: 1 hour 40 minutes, plus freezing time

COOKING TIME: 15-20 minutes

SERVES: 6-8 people

120g/4oz plain chocolate, chopped or grated
600ml/1 pint milk
7 egg yolks
120g/4oz caster sugar

Put the chocolate into a saucepan with a little milk. Stir over a low heat until the chocolate melts and forms a smooth paste. Add the remaining milk. Beat the egg yolks and sugar together until thick and light. Beat into the chocolate milk. Stir continuously over a low heat until thick. Pour the mixture into a bowl and stand over ice. (If you do not have a lot of ice, chill in the refrigerator). Either pour into an ice cream churn and follow the manufacturer's instructions, or pour into ice trays and freeze for 30 minutes. Tip the part-frozen ice cream into a bowl and beat until smooth. Return to the freezer. Repeat this process every 30 minutes, until the ice cream is really thick. Freeze until ready to serve.

Facing page: Pears in Wine. This page: Zuppa alla Romana.

Nougat Ice Cream Cake

PREPARATION TIME:
40 minutes, plus freezing

SERVES: 6-8 people

60g/2oz ground almonds
16 small wafer biscuits
425g/15oz tin pineapple pieces or 225g/
*   8oz crystallized pineapple*
420ml/³/4 pint vanilla ice cream
420ml/³/4 pint chocolate ice cream
120g/4oz plain chocolate, finely chopped
120g/4oz nougat
420ml/³/4 pint whipping cream,
*   whipped*

Grease a 460g/1lb loaf tin and sprinkle the inside with ground almonds. Put 12 of the wafer biscuits around the sides and base of the pan. Drain the pineapple pieces (or chop the crystallized pineapple). Soften the ice creams by placing them in the refrigerator. Spoon the vanilla ice cream into the tin and smooth it down. Add the chopped chocolate to the chocolate ice cream, and ³/4 of the chopped pineapple. Spoon this mixture on top of the vanilla ice cream. Chop the nougat into small pieces and sprinkle it on top of the chocolate ice cream. Cover the chocolate ice cream with the remaining 4 wafer biscuits. Freeze for 3-4 hours, until firm. Spoon the whipped cream over the unmoulded ice cream cake. Decorate with the reserved pineapple. Serve cut into slices.

Strawberries and Oranges

PREPARATION TIME:
15 minutes, plus chilling

SERVES: 6 people

900g/2lbs strawberries
2 oranges
60-90g/2-3oz sugar cubes
60ml/2fl oz Liquore alla Mandarina

Hull and slice the strawberries; peel and slice the oranges. Mash half the strawberries with the sugar cubes and liqueur. Stir in the remaining fruit and chill for one hour. Serve in individual dishes.

Lemon Mousse

PREPARATION TIME: 6-10 minutes

SERVES: 6 people

5 lemons
3 eggs, separated
175g/6oz sugar
15g/¹/2oz gelatine
2 tbsps warm water

Grate the lemons and put the rind in a bowl with the egg yolks and sugar. Beat until stiff. Beat the egg whites until they peak. Dissolve the gelatine in the water and mix with the egg yolk mixture. Beat until the mixture begins to set. Fold in the egg whites. Fill serving glasses with mousse and chill before serving.

Orange Tart

PREPARATION TIME: 30 minutes

COOKING TIME: 25 minutes

OVEN TEMPERATURE:
190°C/375°F/Gas Mark 5

SERVES: 6 people

1 cooked pastry case
2 navel oranges, boiled for 25 minutes
2 egg yolks, beaten
175g/6oz sugar

TO DECORATE
3 navel oranges
Apricot jam, melted

Purée the boiled oranges. Stir in the egg yolks and sugar. Slice the remaining oranges. Fill the pie shell with the orange purée and decorate with slices of orange. Bake in a moderate oven until bubbling. Remove from the oven and brush on melted apricot jam. Return to the oven and bake for a further 10 minutes.

Right: Chocolate Ice Cream (top) and Nougat Ice Cream Cake (bottom).

Strawberries and Oranges (right),
Orange Tart (centre right) and Lemon
Mousse (far right).

Strawberry and Melon Salad

PREPARATION TIME: 25 minutes

SERVES: 4 people

225g/8oz large strawberries, hulled
1 small honeydew melon
Juice of 1 orange
1 tbsp strega

TO DECORATE
Small sprigs fresh mint

Slice the strawberries quite thinly. Halve and de-seed the melon and then scoop it into small balls. Arrange the strawberry slices and melon balls on individual glass plates. Mix the orange juice with the strega and dribble over the fruit. Decorate with mint.

Cherries in Wine

PREPARATION TIME: 5 minutes

COOKING TIME: 10 minutes

SERVES: 6 people

460g/1lb cherries, stoned
1/2 tsp ground cinnamon
4 tbsps sugar
275ml/1/2 pint light red wine

Put the cherries, cinnamon, sugar and wine into a heavy saucepan. Boil slowly. Remove the cherries and boil the liquid until reduced and syrupy. Leave covered for 5 minutes. Serve cold, poured over the cherries.

Caramel Oranges

PREPARATION TIME: 15 minutes

SERVES: 6 people

6 oranges (large and juicy)
175ml/6oz sugar
420ml/15 fl oz water

Peel the oranges. Put the sugar and water in a heavy saucepan. Boil the mixture until it begins to caramelize. Place the oranges in a presentation dish and pour over the liquid caramel. Serve immediately.

This page: Strawberry and Melon Salad. Facing page: Caramel Oranges (top), Blackberry Fluff (centre left) and Cherries in Wine (bottom).

Apricot Mountain

PREPARATION TIME: 20 minutes

COOKING TIME:
4 minutes, or until meringue is brown

OVEN TEMPERATURE:
230°C/450°F/Gas Mark 8

SERVES: 6

About 340g/12oz tinned apricot halves
4-6 tbsps Marsala
3 egg whites
120g/4oz sugar
20cm/8-inch sponge flan case
420ml/³⁄4 pint vanilla ice cream

Strain the apricots and sprinkle them
with the Marsala. Beat the egg whites
until stiff and fold in the sugar. Beat
again until the meringue peaks. Stand
the flan case on a heatproof dish and
sprinkle with a little Marsala. Pile the
apricots onto the cake. Cover the
apricots with a mountain shape of ice
cream. Refreeze until firm. Using the
meringue mixture, quickly cover the
ice cream and the sponge cake base.
Bake immediately until the meringue
is light brown. Serve immediately. For
a very special effect
bury half an egg shell in the top of the
mountain before baking the meringue.
As you serve, fill it with warmed brandy,
ignite and serve flaming.

Blackberry Fluff

PREPARATION TIME: 10 minutes

SERVES: 6 people

460g/1lb blackberries, drained
275g/10oz mascarpone or cream cheese
1 egg white
60g/2oz sugar

Sieve the blackberries. Stir the
blackberry purée into the mascarpone.
Beat the egg white, adding the sugar
slowly until the mixture is stiff. Fold
the egg white into the black-berry
cream. Spoon into individual serving
glasses and serve. A quick and
luscious dessert. Make it in advance,
but in individual glasses. Store in the
refrigerator and serve chilled.

Amaretto Cream

PREPARATION TIME: 10 minutes

SERVES: 4-6

340g/12oz mascarpone or cream cheese
2 tbsps sugar
4 tbsps Amaretto di Saronno
280ml/10 fl oz whipping cream

Beat the cheese until smooth. Add
the sugar and gradually beat in the
cream. Fold in the Amaretto. Pile into
a bowl or individual dishes and chill.

Orange Campari Mousse

PREPARATION TIME:
45 minutes, plus chilling

SERVES: 6 people

1 tsp powdered gelatine
2 medium oranges, washed and dried
90g/3oz icing sugar
2 eggs, separated
3 tbsps Campari
1 tbsp cold milk
150ml/5 fl oz double cream
Orange slices
Mint leaves

Add the gelatine to 2 tbsps of water
in a saucepan. Leave to one side.
Grate the peel of 1 orange. Squeeze
oranges and if necessary make up
juice to 175ml/6 fl oz with water.
Dissolve the gelatine over a low heat.
Stir in the orange juice. Pour mixture
into a bowl, beat in the sugar, egg
yolks, Campari and orange peel. Place
in a fridge until the mixture begins to
the thicken and set. In one bowl, beat
the egg whites until stiff. In another,
whip the milk and cream until thick.
Gradually mix egg whites and cream
alternately into the orange mixture
until totally incorporated. Pour into a
bowl and place in the refrigerator
until firm and set. Serve in glasses,
decorated with orange slices and mint
leaves.

**Left: Apricot Mountain (left) and
Orange Campari Mousse (right).**

Chocolate Crunch

PREPARATION TIME:
20 minutes, plus chilling

MAKES: 460g/1lb loaf

120g/4oz shortbread
120g/4oz firm margarine
90g/3oz sugar
2 tbsps cocoa
1 egg, lightly beaten
60g/2oz whole hazelnuts
60g/2oz sultanas

TO DECORATE
Icing sugar

Line a 460g/1lb loaf tin with cling film. Chop up the shortbread. Brown the hazelnuts and rub off the skins. Put the margarine and sugar into a small saucepan and stir over a low heat until the sugar has dissolved. Stir the cocoa into the mixture and remove from the heat. Stir in the egg, hazelnuts, sultanas and chopped shortbread. Pour the mixture into the lined pan and smooth it level. Chill until set. Dust with icing sugar and serve cut into slices.

This page: Chocolate Crunch. Facing page: Amaretto Cream (left) and Thousand Leaf Almond Cake (right).

Thousand Leaf Almond Cake

PREPARATION TIME: 1 hour

COOKING TIME: 10 minutes for each batch of rounds

OVEN TEMPERATURE: 190°C/375°F/Gas Mark 5

SERVES: 6-8

460g/1lb sugar
340g/12oz butter
2 eggs
300g/11oz plain flour
2 tbsps ground almonds
840ml/1¹/₂ pints double cream, whipped
Icing sugar
Whole almonds

Cut out 12 22cm/9-inch circles of non-stick baking paper. Cream the sugar and butter together and beat in the eggs. Fold in the sifted flour and ground almonds. Divide the mixture into 12 and, using a large palette knife, coat the individual paper rounds with the mixture. Work from the centre outwards with smooth strokes. Wet a baking sheet and bake the rounds. Leave until cool and carefully peel off the paper. When all the rounds are cooked, use them to form layers, spreading each one with whipped cream. Reserve 150ml/5 fl oz of the cream for decoration. Dust the top with icing sugar and decorate with the almonds and cream.

Plums Baked in Red Wine

PREPARATION TIME: 5 minutes

COOKING TIME: 45 minutes

OVEN TEMPERATURE: 150°C/300°F/Gas Mark 2

SERVES: 6

900g/2lbs plums, halved and stoned
120ml/4 fl oz honey
150ml/5 fl oz sweet red wine

Place plums in a baking dish. Spoon over the honey and wine. Cover and bake in a cool oven until the plums are tender. Serve warm or lightly chilled.

Peaches Amalia

PREPARATION TIME: 10 minutes

8 ripe peaches
680g/1¹/₂lbs raspberries
2 tbsps Maraschino
90g/3oz icing sugar

Slice the peaches and place in a serving dish. Add the raspberries and Maraschino. Leave to stand for 1 hour in a cool place. Spoon into individual dishes and sprinkle with icing sugar. Chill and serve with cream.

Stuffed Baked Peaches

PREPARATION TIME: 15 minutes

COOKING TIME: 30 minutes

OVEN TEMPERATURE: 180°C/350°F/Gas Mark 4

SERVES: 6 people

6 large peaches, peeled, halved and stoned
6 macaroons, crushed
45g/1¹/₂oz ground almonds
1 tsp finely grated orange rind
2 egg yolks
3 tbsps butter, cut into small pieces
225g/8 fl oz sweet white wine

Put the peaches on a baking dish, cut side up. Into a small mixing bowl put the crushed macaroons, almonds, orange rind and egg yolks. Mix together and use to fill the peaches. Put a knob of butter on top of each peach. Pour the wine into the baking dish and bake. Serve warm.

Stuffed Oranges

PREPARATION TIME: 15 minutes

SERVES: 8 people

4 large oranges
1¹/₂ tbsps soft brown sugar
1¹/₂ tbsps raisins
1¹/₂ tbsps dates, chopped
1¹/₂ tbsps nuts, toasted and chopped

175ml/6 fl oz double cream
2 tsps icing sugar

Halve the oranges and scoop out the flesh, keeping the shells intact. Chop the flesh, discarding all the pith, and put it in a bowl. Add to the orange flesh the brown sugar, raisins, dates and nuts. Mix well. Scoop the mixture back into the orange halves. Whip the cream with the icing sugar until it forms soft peaks. Spoon this cream on top of the orange mixture. Chill and serve.

Fruit Salad with Ricotta Cheese

PREPARATION TIME: 20 minutes

SERVES: 6 people

90g/3oz cranberries or cherries
90g/3oz raspberries
4 tbsps orange juice
75g/2¹/₂oz sugar
2 tbsps Maraschino cherry
3 kiwi fruit
2 tbsps icing sugar
225g/8oz ricotta cheese

Boil the cranberries or cherries, raspberries and orange juice with the sugar for 5 minutes. Strain the liquid and reserve the fruit. Stir in the Maraschino and cool. Peel and slice the kiwi fruit. Arrange the fruit on individual plates. Stir the icing sugar into the ricotta cheese and place a little on top of each plateful of fruit. Chill. Spoon over the Maraschino liquid to serve.

Facing page: Peaches Amalia (top), Stuffed Oranges (centre) and Plums Baked in Red Wine (bottom).

Marsala Cream

PREPARATION TIME: 15 minutes

SERVES: 6 people

340ml/12 fl oz double cream
4 tbsps sugar
3 tbsps Marsala
4 tbsps honey
3 tbsps lemon juice
3 egg whites
Soft brown sugar
1 packet Amaretti biscuits

Whip the cream, adding the sugar gradually. Fold in the Marsala, honey and lemon juice. Beat the egg whites and fold into the cream. Spoon into serving dishes. Decorate with brown sugar and crumbled Amaretti biscuits.

Chocolate Ravioli

PREPARATION TIME:
30 minutes, plus chilling

MAKES: 25 pieces

100g/4oz roasted almonds
250g/9oz white chocolate, melted

Line a square baking sheet with a rim of foil, making sure that it is smooth and even, with neat corners. Arrange the almonds neatly in one layer. Pour the melted white chocolate evenly over the almonds, so as to cover them completely. Place the sheet in the refrigerator until firm. Cut the ravioli into rows with a knife or ravioli cutter, and then separate each one.

This page: Chocolate Lemon Cake. Facing page: Marsala Cream (top), Stuffed Baked Peaches (centre) and Fruit Salad with Ricotta Cheese (bottom).

Chocolate Nut Torte

PREPARATION TIME:
30 minutes, plus chilling time
MAKES:
1 cake, 18cm/7 inches in diameter

2 tbsps butter
1 tbsp honey
60g/2oz crushed Amaretti biscuits

FILLING
3 tbsps cornflour
1 tbsp cocoa
420ml/15 fl oz milk
150ml/5 fl oz chocolate-flavoured yogurt
1 tbsp hazelnuts, skinned and roughly
    chopped

TOPPING
5 tbsps mascarpone cheese
150ml/5 fl oz double cream, whipped

TO DECORATE
Grated chocolate
8 whole hazelnuts

Melt the butter and honey in a saucepan. Add the crushed Amaretti biscuits and mix well until they are coated with the butter syrup. Press the mixture into the base of an 18cm/ 7-inch fluted flan ring with a removable base. Leave to cool. For the filling, mix the cornflour and cocoa with a little of the milk. Heat the remaining milk until boiling and pour onto the cornflour mixture, stirring constantly. Return the mixture to the pan and return to the heat; simmer for a few minutes until thickened. Remove the saucepan from the heat and stir in the chocolate yogurt and chopped hazelnuts. Pour the mixture over the crisp base. For the topping, mix the cheese with the whipped cream and spread it over the chocolate mixture. Put the flan in the refrigerator and chill until set. Carefully remove the flan ring and decorate with grated chocolate and whole hazelnuts.

This page: Florentines. Facing page:
Chocolate Pistachio Loaf (top) and
Chocolate Nut Torte (bottom).

Chocolate Lemon Cake

PREPARATION TIME: 30 minutes
COOKING TIME: 40-45 minutes
OVEN TEMPERATURE:
180°C/350°F/Gas Mark 4
MAKES: 1 2-lb cake

175g/6oz butter or margarine
175g/6oz soft brown sugar
3 eggs
Grated rind of 1 lemon
225g/8oz self-raising flour
100g/4oz plain chocolate, melted

ICING
175g/6oz butter
450g/1lb icing sugar, sieved
2 tbsps lemon juice

TO DECORATE
Crystallized orange and lemon slices

Grease and line a 1kg/2lb rectangular tin or loaf tin. Cream the butter and sugar together until light and fluffy. Beat in the eggs, one at a time, adding a little flour with each egg. Beat in the lemon rind and remaining flour, and then the chocolate. Pour into the prepared pan. Bake in the oven for 40 45 minutes. Turn out onto a wire rack to cool. To make the icing, put all the ingredients into a mixing bowl and beat with a wooden spoon until well mixed. Cut the cake in half and use half of the butter cream to sandwich the cake together. Spread remaining icing on top of the cake and decorate with crystallized orange and lemon slices.

Almond Tarts

PREPARATION TIME: 10 minutes

COOKING TIME: 10 minutes

OVEN TEMPERATURE:
180°C/350°F/Gas Mark 4

MAKES: 12 tarts

90g/3oz butter
90g/3oz sugar
90g/3oz ground almonds

Beat the butter, sugar and almonds together to a cream. Put 1 tsp of the mixture into each of 12 small patty tins. Bake in a preheated oven for about 10 minutes, or until golden brown. Cool in the tins, but do not allow to set hard before removing to a wire rack. Fresh fruits such as raspberries, peaches or blackberries should be placed on these just before decorating with whipped cream and serving.

Chocolate Pistachio Loaf

PREPARATION TIME: 20 minutes

COOKING TIME: 1¼-1½ hours

OVEN TEMPERATURE:
180°C/350°F/Gas Mark 4

MAKES: 1 450g/1lb loaf

120g/4oz self-raising flour
120g/4oz butter or margarine
60g/2oz caster sugar
60g/2oz plain chocolate, chopped
60g/2oz pistachio nuts, chopped
30g/1oz ground almonds
2 eggs
2 tbsps milk

ICING
175g/6oz plain chocolate, chopped or
  grated
1 tbsp butter

TO DECORATE
A few pistachio nuts, chopped

Grease and line a 450g/1lb loaf tin with greaseproof paper. Put all the cake ingredients in a mixing bowl and beat until they are well mixed. Pour the mixture into the prepared pan. Bake in a preheated oven for 1¼ hours, or until cooked. Turn the cake out of the pan and leave to cool on a wire rack. To make the icing, melt the chocolate in a bowl over a pan of hot water; beat the butter into the chocolate and pour evenly over the cake. Sprinkle with chopped pistachio nuts.

Florentines

PREPARATION TIME: 15 minutes

COOKING TIME: 8-10 minutes

OVEN TEMPERATURE:
180°C/350°F/Gas Mark 4

MAKES: 12

90g/3oz butter
90g/3oz golden syrup
90g/3oz flaked almonds, chopped
30g/1oz plain flour
2 tbsps chopped mixed peel
4 tbsps glacé cherries, chopped
1 tsp lemon juice
100g/4oz plain chocolate, chopped or
  grated

Line a baking sheet with greaseproof paper. Melt the butter and syrup together in a small saucepan. Stir in the almonds, flour, mixed peel, cherries and lemon juice. Put small spoonfuls of the mixture onto the prepared baking sheet. Keep them far apart and flatten with a fork. Bake in a preheated oven for 8-10 minutes. Remove the Florentines carefully to a wire rack to cool. Melt the chocolate in a bowl over a pan of hot water. Spread over the flat side of each Florentine. Place the cookies chocolate sides uppermost and mark the liquid chocolate with wavy lines, using a fork. Leave until set.

Right: Almond Tarts.

Apricot and Walnut Teabread

PREPARATION TIME: 20 minutes
COOKING TIME: 1 hour 30 minutes
OVEN TEMPERATURE: 160°C/325°F/Gas Mark 3
MAKES: 1 loaf

175g/6oz softened butter
175h/6oz light soft brown sugar
3 eggs, beaten
225g/8oz flour
1¹/₂ tsps baking powder
2 tbsps milk
120g/4oz dried apricots, chopped
60g/2oz chopped walnuts

TO DECORATE
2 tbsps clear honey, warmed
Extra chopped dried apricots

Lightly grease a 1kg/2lb loaf tin and line the base with a piece of greaseproof paper. Cream the butter and sugar until light and fluffy. Gradually beat in the eggs, adding a little flour if the mixture shows signs of curdling. Mix in the flour and baking powder, together with the milk, and finally stir in the chopped apricots and nuts. Put the mixture into the prepared loaf tin, smoothing the top level. Bake in the oven for 1¹/₂ hours. If the top of the loaf starts to darken too much, cover it with a piece of foil. As soon as the loaf comes out of the oven, brush the top with the warmed honey and sprinkle with the chopped apricots. Leave to cool in the tin for a few minutes before turning out.

Date and Pistachio Biscuits

PREPARATION TIME: 20 minutes
COOKING TIME: 12-15 minutes
OVEN TEMPERATURE: 190°C/375°F/Gas Mark 5
MAKES: about 12

120g/4oz butter
60g/2oz soft brown sugar
120g/4oz wholemeal flour
60g/2oz ground almonds
90g/3oz stoned dates, chopped
2 tbsps chopped shelled pistachios

TO DECORATE
Chopped shelled pistachios

Work the butter, brown sugar, flour and ground almonds to a soft, smooth dough. Knead lightly, working in the chopped dates and pistachios. Press the mixture into small boat-shaped moulds. Press a few chopped pistachios into the top of each uncooked biscuit. Bake in the oven for 12-15 minutes.

Macaroons

PREPARATION TIME: 20 minutes
COOKING TIME: 20 minutes
OVEN TEMPERATURE: 180°C/350°F/Gas Mark 4
MAKES: 20

225g/8oz caster sugar
150g/5oz ground almonds
1 tbsp rice flour
2 egg whites
Rice paper
20 split almonds

Mix the sugar, almonds and rice flour together. In a separate bowl, beat the egg whites lightly and add the ready-mixed ingredients. Let the mixture stand for 5 minutes. Line a baking sheet with rice paper. Mould the mixture into little balls and place them on the lined baking sheet slightly apart. Gently flatten the macaroons and put an almond on each one. Bake in the oven for 20 minutes, then cool on the baking sheet.

This page: Macaroons. Facing page: Apricot and Walnut Teabread (top) and Date and Pistachio Cookies (bottom).

INDEX